Brian Powell

Their Own
Special Shape

Further approaches to writing
from classrooms around the world

Collier Macmillan Canada, Ltd.

Design and Photography by Michael van Elsen

Collier Macmillan Canada, Ltd.
1125B Leslie Street, Don Mills, Ontario M3C 2K2

SBN: 02.973040.6

Printed and Bound in Canada
54321
80   79   78   77   76

Acknowledgments

The Jacaranda Press (Milton, Australia) — for poem "Aboriginal Charter of Rights" from *We Are Going* by Kath Walker.

Alfred A. Knopf, Inc. (New York, U.S.A.) — for poem "Dreams" from *The Dream Keeper and Other Poems* by Langston Hughes. Copyright © 1932 by Alfred A. Knopf, Inc. and renewed 1960 by Langston Hughes. Reprinted by permission of Alfred A. Knopf, Inc.

Harold Ober Associates Inc. (New York, U.S.A.)—for poem "City: San Francisco" from *The Langston Hughes Reader* by Langston Hughes, published by George Braziller, Inc. Copyright © 1958 by Langston Hughes. Reprinted by permission of Harold Ober Associates Inc.

Project Seven Music, Division of C.T.M.P. Inc. (New York, U.S.A.)—for excerpt from song "Suzanne Takes You Down" by Leonard Cohen (from album *Songs of Leonard Cohen*). Copyright © 1966.

Charles Scribner's Sons (New York, U.S.A.)—for excerpt from *Poems to Solve* by May Swenson.

A.P. Watts and Son (London, England)—for poem "Flying Crooked" from *Collected Poems 1975* by Robert Graves.

Special thanks to the children — Miriam and Rebecca Dalfen, Jacqueline and Anne van Elsen — for their creative artwork.

Canadian Cataloguing in Publication Data

Powell, Brian S., date
Their own special shape

Sequel to Making poetry.

Includes index.
ISBN 0-02-973040-6 pa.

1. Poetry—Study and teaching (Elementary).
2. Children's writings. I. Title.
PN1101.P68   372.6'4   C76-017084-3

Contents

Foreword

"How do I know what I think," the old story has it, "until I hear what I say?" All thinking, apart from meandering meditation, is some kind of saying, of directing language toward an audience, even if the audience is only the other half of one's own heart. And how, we might go on, do I know what I feel until I say what I feel? There are random sensations, but they mean nothing until they are expressed in word or symbol, music or movement.

This book offers a collection of thoughts and feelings of boys and girls throughout the world. Brian Powell has travelled around the world every year for ten years, dropping in on schools, assembling groups of pupils, and bidding them to think and feel and say. What they have said in response to his bidding is laid out here: only a fraction of the enormous talent they have bestowed on him but ample evidence of hearts and minds at work.

Two features of this book are unique and significant. One is that the writing comes from a wide variety of cultures, yet it conveys an intensely personal note. The poems are all different, but in a sense they are all the same. And this prompts the trite but overwhelming reflection that in any culture persons are persons, equal in the fact of difference. Boys and girls growing up in their own culture have to be instructed in a great deal of public and impersonal knowledge, but their humanity really blossoms from their personal observations and individual responses.

The other remarkable quality of the writing collected here is the concentration of attention and expression. Good writing calls for focusing of the senses and of the mind, which interprets sense experiences and selects appropriate words and phrases. By careful sifting of material, these boys and girls are creating powerful poetry.

These two important features of the book shed light on the problem of what it means to be educated, as distinct from merely being trained, or socialized. For instance, as an educated person I cannot deny that I am coloured by my culture. However I always strive to keep my eyes wide-open and to see things for myself. Though I am unable to invent my own unique reality as some of the talk about "creativity" implies, I can stand on my own ground and respond with close attention to the cultural environment around me. This kind of seeing and saying contains the secret of the educative process.

Brian Powell's commentary shows how the concentration is to be stimulated. In essence it is very simple. He *points* young people and provokes their economy of expression. The techniques he describes are not difficult to use; any teacher can learn them from this book.

What is perhaps not so easy for anyone to learn is the total respect for young minds and hearts which Brian Powell brings to his work. He secures this wealth of writing, it must be remembered, in short visits to his schools. He has no time to develop the personal relationships within which education normally takes place; he operates, in a sense, as a stranger. But young writers do not feel him to be a stranger because he approaches them in a subtle spirit of equality, directing them to the reality of their own vision and the validity of their individual message. And this, too, is a secret of the educative process. We teach not by telling, but by causing to see, and by giving confidence that the seeing is true and important. The educated man is the one who, assured of his own grasp of meaning, stands confidently on his own ground.

Harold Loukes,
Reader in Education,
Oxford University.

Preface

The title of this book grew across years and continents. Two springs ago I was in Toowoomba, Queensland, on a radiant May morning. It was such a fine day that I took my class of young men from Downlands College outside onto the upper oval. We sat admiring the sparkling vista of Mount Kynock and the rich Darling Downs. I asked the boys to concentrate on something they hadn't noticed before, and to write a four-line poem about it. James Campbell lay on his back in the grass, and observed the clouds moving slowly overhead. At the end of the period, he handed me his poem:

Cloud

Cloud,
Shifting, moving,
Forming different figures,
Searching for its own special shape.

Doesn't his last line capture the essence of what each one of us is doing every day of our lives?

In the fall of this year I was in Saskatoon, Saskatchewan, at the heart of the golden prairie wheat belt to address the Canadian Council of Teachers of English. I shared James Campbell's poem with a large group. Jean Stinson, an editor at Collier Macmillan, came up to me at the end of the session.

"That last line is a beauty. Couldn't you work it into a title for the new book?"

As I was running through a grain field two hours later—and the falling sun seemed to be setting it aflame—the title struck:

Their Own Special Shape

That's what this book is all about. It has grown out of school visits around the world and belongs to all the people who have always made me feel so welcome, especially the young people. It is to them and their generous teachers that I wish to express my warmest appreciation.

1. Introduction

Learning Goals

What are the learning goals that a teacher using this poetry-making approach might hope to achieve? Four stand out:

Observation

To encourage pupils to use their senses more actively—to observe more closely and to listen more attentively. Pupils need to be taught the skill of making things happen. As an experienced writer has said: "Originality is a good pair of eyes."

Expression

To give pupils training in the skills of expression. Writing is a craft. It requires knowledge of specific techniques and practice in their use. Making poetry can serve as a focus for work in syntax, vocabulary, and almost any form of written expression.

Opportunity for Development of Potential

To give pupils opportunities to develop their abilities. As a young Canadian girl wrote recently in the last line of a poem dedicated to her budgie: "Keep on practising your beauty".

Every young person has gifts to offer others. This book seeks to help individuals to develop their potential, to discover themselves. This is one of its most important aims.

Confidence to Develop Potential

To give pupils a belief in themselves is probably the greatest contribution we can make in our teaching. We should try to show our pupils through the dignity and respect of our manner toward them that each one of them is a unique individual, with a particular contribution to make— his/her own special shape. Such development of self-esteem usually leads the young person on the road to self-discovery, and hence to improved performance in many areas. Jerome Kagan, the prominent Harvard University professor, underlines this point: "The number one factor in school success is to develop the learner's feeling of self-esteem."

The attainment of all these goals— observation, expression, opportunity and confidence to develop potential— through the practice of writing poetry, cannot help but enable pupils to gain a fuller enjoyment of each day.

Setting A Creative Climate

Everyone Can Write

Everybody can have a try at making poetry and receiving personal satisfaction from doing so. One of the most exciting aspects of this creative approach is that we can never tell who is going to derive most from the experience. More than half the fine poems chosen as examples in this book were written by pupils who fell below the half-way mark in their class rankings— the supposedly less able.

Every day in my own working with young people, I receive a large number of poems. Often these are misspelled and badly written on scruffy pieces of paper; yet the names on the papers never fail to elicit comments of amazement from the teachers who know the writers well. One of the beauties of self-expression is that it is not a parrot-task, something that can be learned as a formula can, and regurgitated at the appropriate moment. Expression involves feelings and life experiences, and these, fortunately, are not inseparably linked to intelligence (as measured on intelligence tests) or success on school examinations.

All young people have potential for making poetry. What the slower ones probably require is additional practice in the skills of expression. They need time and encouragement. But they will eventually succeed; and on that day, their smiles of accomplishment will speak louder than a 1000 words.

The Creative Climate

In order that your pupils may feel free and want to produce their best writing, you should try to establish a positive atmosphere in your classroom. This climate will come primarily from two sources: the response of your pupils to one another's work and your own understanding encouragement.

Let's look at each of these areas. It is imperative that your pupils realize that they are all apprentices at the craft of learning to use words. When someone in the class makes a mistake—even if it is an apparently glaring and fundamental one—he/she must not be mocked by the group, for practically all chance of future sincerity on the part of the writer will be lost. You must encourage your pupils to be tolerant of one another's opinions and weaknesses of expression. Without this atmosphere of respect, pupils will not feel free to write what they really believe. In that case you might as well not even start.

As for yourself, I would suggest that you strive to give encouragement throughout but especially in the early stages when your pupils are making a leap of faith by sharing parts of themselves with you. There is no need to be hypocritical in this. If a young writer hands me a five-line poem in which four of the lines contain little merit at the moment, I probably say nothing about these, but concentrate on the one line that shows promise. I encourage him/her with this line, and try to reinforce what has been done well. Later on in our relationship, perhaps even weeks or months later when we have developed a stronger mutual understanding and when the pupil realizes that whatever I am suggesting is done within a framework of respect, then I can make stronger constructive criticisms and he/she will be able to accept them. Get to know each individual with whom you are working as far as this is possible, and hence try to offer your suggestions on an individual and personal basis. At all costs avoid crushing growing seeds of trust.

Nothing inhibits the development of a creative class more than teachers, examiners, or pupils who are impatient for instant results. Curriculum planners may suggest that unless a certain percentage of any class produces poems of literary merit, then the exercise of trying to make poems is a waste of time. Can we measure the result of any writing session by what the pupils have been able to get on their pages in a few restricted minutes? Does writing operate that way for anyone? The following letter—a very typical one, in fact—from a student suggests the answer:

"Dear Mr. Powell

My name is Julie. You probably don't remember me, but you came to our school in Hobart, Tasmania last May and spoke to us about writing poetry. On that day I wasn't really in the mood and I wasn't able to do much in class. But last weekend I went for a walk in the bush and I saw a spider web. I remembered that form you suggested so I sat down and wrote this poem. I thought you might like to see it...."

Surely, this is a large part of the *result* of a poetry-writing session held many months before. Should we as teachers expect to see seeds flower in front of our eyes— FAST?

What concerns me more than anything else about any of the sessions I conduct is the quality of time we share. Were the young people genuinely involved in what we were talking about? Did they have an idea clearly in their minds, and some definite guidelines to help them some day to develop it? Might they want to continue at some later time to explore what we discussed?

Writing effectively has never been easy or quick. Making a poem takes time and patience. If it could be produced effortlessly, most of the joy and challenge of creation would be lost.

Discovering Your Best

Education is people business. At its essence it is concerned with relationships among human beings, with loving and sharing love. While machines are replacing people in many areas today, no machine 'can ever replace the impact of one life upon another— the closeness of contact that has characterized inspired teaching since the time of the Greeks. No other enterprise makes greater demands on those involved in it to discover their best, and to give it. No other profession reaps greater rewards.

Much has been written about the characteristics of the good teacher. Qualities are mentioned such as a liking for young people, an enthusiasm for living and learning, a sense of humour, a knowledge of the subject, innovative capacity, a sense of the dramatic, and personal depth. This might seem like a formidable list to individuals starting a teaching career and wondering whether or not they have the potential for it. However such persons should not worry needlessly. Provided that they really want to become teachers and are ready to work at it, they can largely be *made*.

The British National Theatre School takes eager apprentices almost literally off the streets, and, in time, makes presentable actors of them. In the same way, all a teacher really needs at the outset is a liking of the young, and a desire to learn with them and from them in every situation. In all other respects a good teacher, like a good actor, can be made. By continually striving to help our students develop their sensibilities and self-esteem, we go a long way toward maximizing our own potential.

Structure of the Book

Their Own Special Shape is a book about writing and self-discovery. *English Through Poetry Writing* and *Making Poetry* are the two predecessors in the series. You might find them interesting resource tools; however they are not essential to using this book.

Both these earlier works are more highly structured with specific chapters labelled "Form" and "Content." Here, instead, I am offering 32 flexible writing triggers to be adapted to your own classroom situation. Use them as you might pick cards from a deck. If your pupils need more specific guidance with form, refer back to *Making Poetry*.

As with all ideas, the ones presented here are an advance on my earlier ones, and I hope that you and your pupils will find them stimulating. I have worked hard to make them of universal appeal to pupils of all ages from upper elementary to the top levels of high school. I object to attempts at categorizing these triggers by age groups. Young writers simply bring their own experiences to them. Their age doesn't really matter. Let us use these ideas to break down barriers of age and to help our pupils transcend classroom walls.

Apart from this more unlabelled approach, I have added a further dimension to this book not found in its two predecessors. At the end of most of the Trigger sections I select one poem for particular comment. How and why was it made? Are there any human interest or topical details you should know about it? My more analytic comments I reserve for Chapter 4 on "Making a Poem."

As the anchor of this book I have used approximately 200 poems of young people drawn from 114 different schools throughout the world. The poems come to you in their original state as submitted by the student. I have not tampered with their distinctive quality in any way.

One is tempted to become sentimental about travels and experiences. Every one of the poems I have ever received means something to me; it has a specific story attached to it. I would enjoy sharing all of them with you. Since this is impossible, discrimination is vital here, as with the showing of slides. Consequently I have chosen a wide variety of sample pieces at all levels of refinement. Since taste is such an individual matter I leave it up to you to decide which poems are better than others. All I have attempted is to show as clearly as possible some of the working of the creative process as it has developed in the minds of young writers.

In order for you to get the most practical value out of this book I present a "Typical Class Session" in Chapter 2. A more complex sample session appears at the beginning of Chapter 4.

What makes any school a potentially creative place? In Chapter 5 I isolate three core qualities and four additional elements, all of which facilitate a positive atmosphere for poetry writing. At the end of the chapter I include a list of 19 schools from various countries that, in my opinion, have made outstanding, creative contributions to education.

As a tribute to youthful ingenuity, in the Appendix I present more poems for your enjoyment and for class discussion. There is also a list of the 114 schools from which the poems in this book are derived.

I am hopeful that teachers using the ideas in this book have enough ease with the approach to treat it more as a guide than a rigid formula. I am counting on you to adapt any of the suggestions made on these pages to suit your classroom needs and situation. Don't try to follow them slavishly as a text going from A to B to C— and then write to me saying "It doesn't work." I was disappointed recently to receive a letter from a teacher in an inner city area telling me that my section on nature has been a failure. In such a situation I would expect it to be a failure. Probably her kids had never seen a tree or a blade of grass. She should probably have started with alley cats, garbage cans, or fire escapes—or wherever the experience of her kids lay at that moment. We must never forget that absolutely anything can be a trigger, especially those objects that are closest at hand.

I hope you find *Their Own Special Shape* useful and stimulating. Enjoy your journey through its pages.

2. Typical Class Session

A typical classroom period of poetry writing might have the following stages:

Brief Introduction by the Teacher

During this five to ten minute stage, outline the form to be attempted using the blackboard if possible. Read several examples to give your pupils some ideas on which to build. It is probably wise to read a range of examples here, not just the best ones you have received. Pupils could be discouraged before they even begin—"I could never write one as good as that"—if you read them outstanding pieces only. Better that they start to write with the feeling "I can make a poem better than that one."

The Writing Itself

During this stage, your pupils should work in silence, and concentrate on their own subjects. This quiet time during the actual writing is something on which I insist. Making a poem is an individual thing, and hence chatting or exchanging ideas during the time for creation is disruptive. Group discussion or oral preparation should take place before, but not during, the actual writing.

Your pupils will obviously work at varying speeds. Some will finish more quickly than others. These I would encourage either to rework their original, or perhaps to try another one if time permits. At any rate they should remain quiet until the time for reading.

The Reading of Poems

During the closing stages of most periods, give your pupils an opportunity to read aloud the pieces they have just made. This occasion will reinforce their efforts and should give them further immediate pleasure. I would never force anyone to read who does not want to do so. Younger kids are usually quick to volunteer. Older pupils may be more reticent. After you have gotten to know your classes, a relationship of trust should develop that will prompt your pupils to share their writing with you. Don't try to rush this moment however.

Something to Eat

A number of teachers have written to ask me how a typical period of poetry writing would proceed. I am reluctant to attempt such an outline because I want each one of you to develop your own approach to these ideas. However, to give you a general idea I now present the selection "Something to Eat," which amounts to a tape reproduction of a typical session. In case you want more exposure to a typical class session, there is another sample, more assessment-oriented, at the beginning of the evaluation chapter (four).

Teacher: Girls and boys, today I'd like to suggest that we try a poem about something we all enjoy doing— eating. *(Sighs of delight!)* What's your favourite thing to eat?

Class: *(assorted volunteers).*
Hamburgers.
French fries with ketchup.
Lemon pie.
Strawberry milk shakes.
Pepperoni pizza.

Teacher: Good stuff. Everybody seems to have a favourite, several in fact. Charlie (a *rather rotund, extrovert at the back*), you seem to like everything that's been mentioned! *(Laughs all around.)*

Charlie: Teacher, today you are right on my wave length!

Teacher: I said we were going to try a poem about your favourite thing to eat. Your poem will need to have some kind of structure. I suggest you try a five-line piece like this:

(Now use the blackboard and draw five lines in this fashion.)

———————————————————————

———————————————————————

———————————————————————

———————————————————————

———————————————————————

Each of these lines we are going to use for one of the five senses. We've talked about them before but what are the five senses? Put up your hands.

Kathy: Touch or feel.

John: Smell.

George: Sight.

Mary: Sound or hearing.

Julie: Balance.

Teacher: A good idea, Julie. Is balance actually one of the five we normally think of, or could we include it with touch or feel perhaps?

Julie: Yes, we could include it there. What I really wanted to say was taste. I guess I didn't think about it because it's so obvious with something to eat.

Teacher: Good. We've got our five then. Let's put each one of them opposite a line in our poem so we have a framework for our writing. Remember, you don't have to put your five in this order. Arrange them in whatever order you think best suits your subject.

(At this stage fill in on the blackboard the five senses as proposed.)

Touch   _____

Smell   _____

Sight   _____

Sound   _____

Taste   _____

(At this point add to the framework on the board a sixth line with the caption "Subject?.")

Subject   _____?_____

Teacher: Now, I don't want you to tell us what you are writing about until this last line . . . here. After you have done your piece, you are going to read it to us, and we'll see if we can guess what your subject is. Let's make this a kind of contest. If we can guess what your topic is, you've probably picked accurate words to describe it. If we can't guess, you may have to look again at how you have written it or perhaps we're just poor guessers. Get the idea?

John: Suppose I can't think up a line for every sense? Maybe my subject has no smell.

Teacher: Good question, John. Don't worry about getting all five senses. If you can't think of something for one or two of them— try your best of course— it doesn't matter. See if you can get three lines anyway. Then we'll have a better chance of guessing what you've written about.

Kathy: Do the lines have to rhyme?

Teacher: You know what we've said before, Kathy. A poem doesn't ever need to rhyme, unless you really want it to. Often when we're trying to get rhyme, we put in words that don't really make sense, but they go with the word

21

above. This isn't really good writing. Please don't worry about rhyme unless you are very keen to have it.

Julie: How long should the lines be?

Teacher: That's a good question, Julie. I'd prefer that you try to keep them reasonably short, perhaps only two, three, or four words long. Remember we said that poetry is usually tighter, more concise than prose. Where a sentence probably stretches from side to side of your page, a poem may take up much less of your line. I always like that expression of the Chinese who say that the best poetry writing is that which is "trimmed to the bone." We all talk and write too much anyway, don't we?

(There are various audible and inaudible class reactions.)

Charlie: You said something about rhythm last time we wrote. I didn't quite get it.

Teacher: Thanks, Charlie. I think that was near the end of the class when Sue read her piece. We didn't really have time to finish talking about it.

Rhythm is to poetry what beat is to music. You enjoyed that Elton John concert last weekend because you said his group had great beat. Poetry needs a beat too. We call it rhythm, and there can be many kinds of rhythm just as music can have many different beats. Try to keep your rhythm tight. Say your poem over to yourself in your head as you are making it. I think you'll be able to tell what sounds best. Don't get it cluttered.

As an example let's put up that poem of Sue's again. Do you remember it? She did that two-line piece on the "Oak."

(At this stage write the poem on the board.)

Oak
A rough hand
Looming against the sky.

Sue: That was my first version. But when I read it out loud, I felt the second line was too long; it had too many syllables in it. So I cut out the word "the." I like it better that way.

Teacher: Thanks, Sue. I agree with you. See, Charlie, Sue listened to her own second line and felt it was a little cluttered for sound, so she trimmed it. That's what rhythm is about. I think you'll hear your own rhythm, but this is a big subject. We'll talk about it again as we go along.

Teacher: Any more questions? . . . . Good. I think we're just about ready to write then. But first, let me read you several pieces done by other pupils. This will give you an idea of what others have done before you begin. See if you can tell me what they have written about. Remember it's something to eat. Don't shout if you think you have the answer. Put up your hand so that everyone can get a chance to guess. What is this?

Stringy with little pieces of meat;
Spicy and hot;
The tender smell of herbs and cheese;
Hard to get on a fork.

Fred: *(with many other hands waving).* Spaghetti—that's easy.

Teacher: You're right, Fred. It was easy, probably because the writer did a good job in describing each of the senses. Did you notice the way each of the lines concentrated on a different sense: sight, taste, smell, and touch? Here's a more difficult one. Tell me exactly what it is.

A mountain of white;
Cold and soft;
Dripping with sticky brown liquid;
Glowing red at the top.

Joe: *(pausing).* A volcano?

(An explosion of laughter.)

Teacher: Joe, that might be a good guess but it has to be
            something to eat.

Kathy: I think it's a sundae.

Teacher: What kind of sundae, Kathy?

Cathy: Caramel.

George: No sir, not caramel; chocolate.

Teacher: Why chocolate, George?

George: The writer said "brown" liquid. I wouldn't call caramel,
            brown. I'd call it more like golden.

Teacher: Good work, George. You listened to the word clues
            well. Here's another harder one.

            Round and white with many layers
            It tastes hot and unbearable
            You'd better not inhale;
            Smooth and slippery to the touch.

Class: *(only one or two hands going up).* That's hard. . . .

Teacher: Let me give you a hint. I'll do it for you in mime. Here's
            the subject on my left hand.

*(There follows a mimed interpretation of cutting an onion in two
with the resultant flowing of tears and the handkerchief to the
rescue!)*

John: I've got it—an onion.

Class: That's a good one.

Teacher: Notice the way the writer told us about smell with the
            line "You'd better not inhale." Now, here's one final
            example. It's my favourite, I think. This one was done for
            me by a boy in Hawaii. I had visited his school and gave

his class the idea we are thinking about today. They all wrote quietly for five or ten minutes, and then handed in their pieces. I couldn't believe it when I read this first line.

(Now write the line on the board.)

XLOMPVARSBTMWYATSOPY

What do you think it describes? When I first saw it, I thought maybe the boy was writing in Polynesian or writing about some Hawaiian dish I had never heard of.

I'll give you a hint. This line describes the sight of something to eat. You've all had it. If you can get this, you go to the head of the class.

Mary: *(pausing):* Alphabet Soup.

(Reactions of recognition and amazement.)

Teacher: Wonderful, Mary. What a guess! I never did get it myself. The rest of the Hawaiian boy's poem went like this:

> XLOMPVARSBTMWYATSOPVY
> Bright orange;
> Scorching hot;
> Gurgling of water boiling;
> Tomatoes, potatoes, beans;
> ALPHABET SOUP.

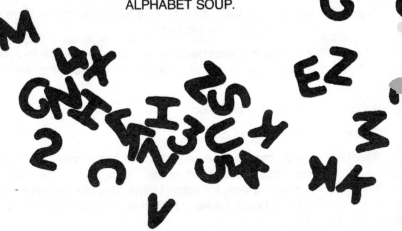

Isn't it a beauty? I think it's my favourite up to now. You all have a piece of paper in front of you. I'll give you five or ten minutes now to do your own poem. Remember it's on something to eat; anything you want to pick. If you finish one, go ahead and try a second one. PLEASE DON'T TALK or look at one another's pieces. If there's noise in the room, you won't be able to concentrate on your own idea. At the end of our writing time, I'd like a few of you to read your pieces aloud, and we'll see if we can guess your subjects. Pick your words carefully, and have a go now.

(Five to ten minutes pass. The pupils work quietly. If there are any questions at this time, I try to answer them individually; but I really discourage discussion here. They know what they are trying to do. Some of the quicker pupils get more than one piece done.)

Teacher: I'm excited to see that most of you have got at least one done. Would anyone like to read so we could try to guess it?

(A number of hands go up, waving enthusiastically.)

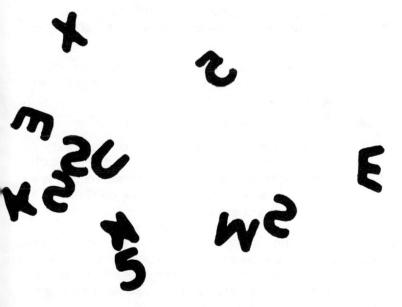

Teacher: Thanks, Kathy. Let's hear yours. Don't read too quickly, please. Remember, we haven't heard your piece yet. And make it loud enough so everyone can hear. Don't tell us the subject. We'll guess.

Kathy: Thick creamy foam;
                    Cool, refreshing taste;
                    Slippery liquid stream;
                    Snow white.

Joe: A vanilla milk shake; that was easy.

Teacher: Is he right, Kathy?

Kathy: He's right. *(Agreement all around.)*

Teacher: Good guess Joe, and well written, Kathy. You picked your words carefully.

(At this stage, a number of other poems should be read and guesses attempted. Some points of writing technique could be stressed, particularly when members of the class have difficulty with their guesses. Any advice offered should always be given in a constructive and encouraging tone at the very end of the period.)

Teacher: You've really done well today. I'm proud of you. How about trying a couple of other pieces like these for our next writing session?

(Generally enthusiastic and approving comments.)

Good. Well, take some time at home or over the weekend, and see what you can do. Next period we'll hear a lot of them read, and we might even copy a few on the board so that we can study the good results. Thanks again and see you then.

Epilogue: Obviously, no class would go exactly like this one, and there would probably be more interplay and comments than I have been able to include here. If the general format of this section has been helpful, however, then it has served its purpose. Take it, and make it your own.

3. Triggers to Creativity

Moods of the Moon

The North American Indians spoke of the months of the year by referring to characteristics of the moon. For instance, they might have called February, "the hunger moon," or March, "the moon of melting snows." They tried to capture the spirit of the month in their one-line statements.

Ask your pupils to think of several months of the year—all twelve if they have time. They are to invent a single-line image about each one which must somewhere contain the word *moon*. Their images should attempt to capture the mood of the particular time of year. After your pupils have created their images, they might like to illustrate each one, or even make a collage of all twelve months together. Here are a few examples written by young people and presented in calendar order:

January   The moon of the dying deer.
             The moon of the freezing blanket.
             The moon of frozen fullness.

February   The long moon.
             The moon of the twilight star.

March   The moon of the angry winds.
             The moon of windy branches.

April	The moon of the early showers. The moon of returning life. The moon of the rainy sky.
May	The moon of the swimming fish. The budding moon.
June	The moon of the stinging insects. The moon of the bullfrog's song.
July	The moon of dancing flowers. The moon of the crying loon.
August	The moon of the morning dew. The moon of the angry sun.
September	The moon of the golden harvest. The moon of burning leaves. The moon of plenty.
October	The moon of ghosts and goblins. The moon of the fleeing birds. The moon of fiery foliage.
November	The moon of the first snows. The grey moon.
December	The moon of great gifts. The moon of the dying sun. The moon of the bitter land.

The exercise of trying to capture the spirit of a month in one line presents an intriguing challenge. Young writers will realize that many names and expressions in current usage grew in this same way. For instance, the pop group "Three Dog Night" takes its name from the fact that shepherds used to sleep with their dogs around them for warmth. Hence a one-dog night was not too cold, but a three-dog night was severe.

Another illustration is the expression "a four-shovel winter." The North American Indians used to say that a winter with little snow was a one-shovel winter—and so on in depth of snowfall up to four.

Distillation

The Chinese claim that the most effective writing is "trimmed to the bone." By this they suggest that all unnecessary words be eliminated. The Japanese through their traditional form, the haiku* also admire conciseness.

Ask you pupils to compose a short piece—four lines long at most—in which their aim is to capture the heart of a situation in as few words as possible. Show them that tightness of expression, particularly when they are trying to write poetry, is a virtue.

The Moon

The moon—
'We'll get there soon'
They said:
They did.

(G.C., Putney School, Putney, U.S.A.)

Crowd

People,
Everywhere I listen
Voices completely surround me—
Yet I am alone.

(R.W., Punahou School, Honolulu, Hawaii)

Rhyming

Rhyming—
A matter of timing;

(M.P., Riverdale High School, Montreal, Canada)

*A three-line, seventeen-syllable poem.

Star

My light has travelled centuries to meet your eye,
And you don't even stop to wonder.

(T.V., Putney School, Putney, U.S.A.)

Spirit

Christmas morning;
Presents were open —
Hearts weren't.

(I.B., Pittwater House Grammar School,
Collaroy, Australia)

Blindness

My eyes are in darkness all the time;
My fingers are my sun.

(George S., Sir Winston Churchill High School,
Montreal, Canada)

George, who wrote this last poem, is a sighted boy. His inspiration
for the piece came when I showed his class a poem written in
braille by a blind pupil. George took the piece of cardboard with
the braille on it, closed his eyes, and carefully traced the raised
patterns of the letters with his fingertips. After thinking about his
experience, he wrote the two-line poem which appears above.

Solve a Poem

A poem is a package of words. If well-written, it must have been put together with care, and so will require similar patience in the undoing. Listen to what May Swenson says in the Introduction to her delightful book *Poems to Solve*: "A poem read for the first time can offer the pleasure of opening a wrapped box. There is the anticipation of untying an intriguing knot of words, of unloosing all their intimations like loops, of lifting out—as if from under cover— an unexpected idea or fresh sensation. Solving a poem can be like undoing a mysterious package."

Ask your pupils to make a number of poems to solve. These should be short—five lines long at most—and should contain distinctive and accurate clues. When all the pupils in your group have written, let them guess one another's subjects. This could take the form of a poetry quiz, and will provide a test of their control of words. What subjects do the following pieces describe?

On finding sugar, they come in numbers;
Departing in a line, fully loaded,
They rub their noses against each other.
(P. Domun, Royal College, Curepipe, Mauritius)
Answer: Ants

It makes its black smear across
the countryside;
Ugly but useful,
Buzzing with its metal bees.
(Peter Miller, Bilton Grange School, Dunchurch, England)
Answer: Highway

Green splinters,
Sharp pointed blades.
(T.L., Lyndon Institute, Lyndonville, U.S.A.)
Answer: Pine Needles

Finely-shaped head
Painted ears pricked, listening—
A living statue of concentration.
(Katie Fitzgerald, Girton Girls School, Adelaide, Australia)

Answer: Cat

Up, down,
In, out,
To and fro—
Full of cold salt.

(Kathryn Lees, Girton Girls School,
Adelaide, Australia)

Answer: Wave

As an extension of the above idea, let your pupils make several poetic riddles. Most young people have had some experience with riddles, which basically are word puzzles. Remind them that the clues they give should not be too obvious. At the same time, they must be accurate and not ambiguous. These riddles might extend to eight or ten lines. Here are several examples as a start:

It is used every day,
Whether going in or out;
It is shiny and comes in
    luminous colours
which often wear out;
If your hand slips on it,
It can't do its job.

(G.L., Cardinal Newman High School,
Montreal, Canada)

Answer: Doorknob

It comes from an animal,
    and is filled with flesh and bones;
Sometimes it is badly misued;
It can cause great pain when it is too small.

(A.G., Riverdale High School, Montreal, Canada)
Answer: Shoe

It is black, round, and comes in many sizes;
It has walls, and helps to carry things;
If it is neglected, it can kill and maim
It is no use if not filled with gas.

(R.N., Ashfield School, Nottingham, England)

Answer: Tire

They are white and used every day;
Most people have them, but a few don't;
Sometimes they are covered with metal;
They move up and down.

(T.S., Sir Winston Churchill High School, Montreal, Canada)

Answer: *Teeth*

It is worn in a certain country,
   and seems to make other nations laugh;
It has stripes and squares of various colours;
The big question is always—
What is underneath it?

(Miss McGhee, Thomas d'Arcy McGee Annex, Montreal, Canada)

Answer: *Kilt*

Learning to use words need not be a dull exercise. It should include all the excitement of a game.

Specific Frameworks

Here are two forms with which your pupils might like to experiment:

Four-Line Reaction Model

In the first line name the subject, either in one word or a few. In the second line describe the action of the subject, likewise in a word or in more detail. In the third line make a simile describing the subject, and in the fourth line give your reaction to the subject. Here are two versions—one longer, the second more concise—of a poem on a black cat.

	Black Cat	
Subject	Black cat so lithe,	Black cat,
Action	Prowling among cans in a half-lit lane,	Prowling,
Simile	Like a sable-coated, symbol-carrying shadow,	Like a shadow,
Reaction	I want to run and hide.	I'm scared.

Here are some other illustrations of this model:

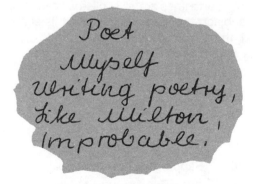

Poet
Myself
writing poetry,
Like Milton,
Improbable.

(C.S., Macdonald
College of Education,
Montreal, Canada)

Water

Water,
Running over smooth stones,
Like shimmering silver
I'm thirsty.

(C.M., Dunton
High School,
Montreal, Canada)

Barracuda

**Barracuda,
Chasing helpless fish;
Like a sly fox;
Run for your life.**

(Thomas A., St. Benedict's School,
Harbour Island, Bahamas)

Harbour Island is a sun-baked, beach-surrounded dot of land two miles wide and five miles long lying just off Nassau in the Bahamas. Fishing is one of the chief occupations of the people there, and each day after school the children gather on the wharf to watch the boats come in. Thomas knows the sea.

Simile Model

This five-line piece starts by naming the subject in its first line. The second, third, and fourth lines are all similes written about different aspects of the subject: the second line, about its sight, the third, about its sound, the fourth, about its action.

The final line of the piece contains a conclusion.

		Evening Rain
Subject		Evening rain,
Similes:	Sight	Glittering like broken glass,
	Sound	Rapping like crinkling foil,
	Action	Falling like a raid of bullets
Conclusion		I'm wet.

(P.V., Westmount High School, Montreal, Canada)

Ice

Ice,
Shiny like a mirror;
Creaking like old wood;
Slippery as a freshly waxed floor;
Watch your step.

(C.M., Dorval High School,
Montreal, Canada)

Puck

Puck,
Black as midnight;
Silent as a shadow;
Speeding like a bullet;
It hurts.

(Michael D., Cardinal Newman High
School, Montreal, Canada)

Michael, who wrote this last poem, is the goalie for Cardinal
Newman's championship ice hockey team. He is writing from
personal experience—always the most direct source of inspiration.

Open Your Eyes—
The Eureka Experience

Effective expression has its foundation in close observation. If our eyes and ears are open, we can feed our minds on ideas about which to write. Observation has far-reaching implications; it is fundamental to nearly all careers and walks of life.

However, we all tend to be careless about observation unless we work at it. Observing well is a conscious process. It demands our full attention.

Ask your pupils to recall any situation in which they have had the Eureka experience—the sudden recognition of the wonder of something they had not noticed before. Ask them to write a short poem about this situation. As an illustration, read this piece by a teaching friend of mine who used to walk to and from school every day down a country road enclosed by oak trees. Although he had made the trip many times, he had never really noticed the trees. One day, however, after a violent thunderstorm that left the sky black, a single shaft of sunlight broke through the darkness and fell directly on the trunk of a large oak. My friend stopped short, and soon after wrote the following poem:

> *I never saw an oak tree,*
> *Until the other day;*
> *Its arms of knotted power, black*
> *Against a sky of gray:*
> *Then burst the sun,*
> *And on its bark*
> *A coat of amber lay.*

(Jeff Campbell, Putney School, Putney, U.S.A.)

Ask your pupils to try to recall a similar happening from their own experience. Let them write about it in eight lines or less. If they have not already had the Eureka experience, ask them to concentrate in the days ahead on making it happen.

Here is a poem written at Iolani School in Hawaii by a boy who is a champion surfer. He has observed the waves closely.

Wave

Advancing, building,
A glistening wall of fluid glass:
It shakes its white head and falls—
Thundering.
(J.M., Iolani School, Honolulu, Hawaii)

Enjoy the detail in these other poems by young writers:

Spider Web

Glistening
Delicate
A shawl of finest threads
Shimmering
(Chris Y., Punahou School,
Honolulu, Hawaii)

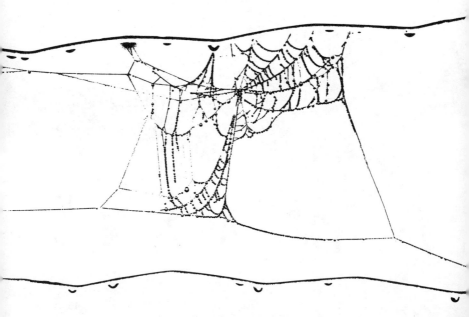

Oily Puddle

Thin slick on water
Oily rainbow in the sun:
Shattered by a booted foot:
A thousand oily colours

**(K.T., Mount Royal High School,
Saskatoon, Canada)**

Moor

Vast wild expanse of moor,
Bitten by wind and frost;
Rocky crags;
Lone foal.

*(Andrew Webber, Bryanston School,
Dorset, England)*

Low Tide

Half rotten cocoanut;
Retreating tinted crab;
Watersnakes,
Smell,
Low tide in a mangrove swamp.

*(Jan Sutherland, Friends School,
Hobart, Australia)*

Jan had just enjoyed a two-week holiday on the islands of New Caledonia. At sunset she used to sit on the waterfront and absorb the sights and sounds there. Her poem presents a collage of the South Pacific twilight scene. The images she has chosen form a picture that is realistic even for those who have never visited the area.

Illustrate a Poem

The idea for a poem can come from anywhere, at any time. Probably people who are commonly termed "creative" would attribute much of their inspiration to close observation. They pay attention to the things around them.

In this section, ask your pupils to link the verbal and the visual. Ask them to write a short poem—four lines long at most—in which the final line has a strong sight impact. It should almost jump off the page and strike the reader's eye much as a picture would. Tell your pupils before they begin that they will have to illustrate their last line. Knowing that they are going to have to draw it should help them form a vivid image of their subject.

When they can train themselves to use their eyes as photographers do, then young writers are conditioning themselves to see inspiration in everything around them, like in waves crashing on the shore or a blast furnace working at night. Stress the fact that their illustrations need not be of high artistic standard. The important lesson here is that they look before they write.

Metal

The metal is there,
Ready to mine;
How do we get it?
Explosion.

(Michael Paton, The King's School,
Parramatta, Australia)

Gum

The great gum tree
Standing out in the cold;
Last summer its leaves were bright and green;
Now it's bare.

(T. Barton, Downlands College, Toowoomba, Australia)

Drought

Cattle dying in despair;
Nothing left but bones and dust.
(Michael Bishop, Warwick High School,
Warwick, Australia)

Sweat

The wind is dead;
The air is moist;
The trail leads to the sun.

(T.P., Hawaii Preparatory Academy,
Kamuela, Hawaii)

Frost

It forms on windows
White and Clear—
Patterns.

(M.J., St. Michael's School,
Moose Jaw, Canada)

This last poem was written on the Canadian prairies by
eleven-year-old Michael from Moose Jaw, Saskatchewan. It was
made on a very cold March day,—22° below zero C—with a strong
wind blowing. As I entered Michael's classroom I was impressed by
nature's designs etched on all the windows. We discussed them,
and then I asked the pupils to write about frost. Michael's last line,
the single word "patterns," has impact because it enables every
listener to establish his own visual image of the shapes traced on
the pane.

Sound Variations

Poetry is partly sense, partly sound. Many are the variations and combinations that make up the sound ingredient. Give your pupils experience with some or all of the following suggestions:

Exercises With Non-Words

A six-year-old boy when asked for a definition said, "Poetry is when words sing." Suggest to your pupils that they make up words in their own private language to substitute for a known word like *moonlight.* The words they invent should sing such as:

> lunious
> shalowa
> noorwahm
> malooma

Let them make up war words, animal words, industrial words, and so on—arranging them in order from the smallest to the largest sound.

Once they have tried a number of these exercises, they should be able to suggest their own ideas. Let them try to make a poem based almost entirely on sound. It need make no logical sense and might be constructed exclusively from their own newly-coined non-words.

Car With A Flat Tire

Haree, haree,
Haroomm—
Blomp, blomp,
Fring,
Pussttt.

(J.G., Sir Winston Churchill High School, Montreal, Canada)

Railroad Train

Camel-a-lot, camel-a-lot,
Adel go friedel,
Camel-a-lot;
Camel-a-lot, camel-a-lot;
Adel go friedel,
Camel-a-lot.

(P.V., Carmel High School, Carmel, U.S.A.)

Other Variations

Give your pupils some writing experience with other sound devices such as repetition, rhyme, and onomatopoeia. Let them try to make a poem which focuses on each of them.

Repetition

Trampoline Class

Bouncing, bouncing,
Up and down;
Knee drop, seat drop,
Swivel round;
Bouncing, bouncing,
into the air,
higher and higher,
until you don't care:
Bouncing, bouncing,
Now do a flip;
Your turn's almost up,
So come down and sit.

(L.K., Otter Valley High School, Brandon, U.S.A.)

Dancing

There he is out on the floor,
Moving, moving;
Shuffling his feet till he can't anymore
Moving, moving;
Rocking, rolling, contorting his limbs,
Moving, moving
Gyrating, twisting; he can't anymore—
Moving.

(P.C., Horace Mann School, New York City, U.S.A.)

Rhyme

Noon

Shady, sleepy, lazy noon,
Murmuring bees and a mother's croon;
Cooing of doves in a motionless elm;
And an ancient old skipper
As he dreams of the helm.
(Ian Peterson, St. John's School, Selkirk, Canada)

Onomatopoeia

Frequently the sound movement of a piece can be made to flow as the subject might flow. As an example read this poem by Robert Graves:

Flying Crooked

The butterfly, a cabbage-white
(His harvest idiocy of flight)
Will never now, it is too late
Master the art of flying straight,
Yet has—who knows so well as I?—
A just sense of how not to fly:
He lurches here, and here by guess,
And God, and hope, and hopelessness.
Even the aerobatic swift
Has not his flying-crooked gift.

Somehow the very sound movement of this poem seems appropriate to the flying crooked aerobatics of the butterfly.

Let your pupils experiment with the following model:

Life is Real

Bronze on bronze,
Steel on steel,
Clang, crash
and life is real;
No lying in a feather bed,
Living off milk and doctoral bread;
Clang, crash,
Steel on steel
Pain is here
And life if real.

(T.S., St. John's School, Selkirk, Canada)

Combinations

Ask your pupils to make a poem that contains a combination of sound devices.

Ivy

Ivy crashes in the fall
Tumbling in rivers
                    down
                         the
                              wall;
The grass is blue;
The sky is green;
And all the leaves
Are left unseen.
Pastoral mumbles, the meadow heath,
And the down wind up comes over neath;

Ivy crashes in the fall,
Tumbling in rivers
                    down
                         the
                              wall.

(P. O'Brien, Phillips Exeter Academy, Exeter, U.S.A.)

To a Musical Tune

Ask your pupils to try to write a poem that could be sung to the tune of some familiar piece of music, perhaps a hit-parade number, popular melody, or hymn.

Here is a poem written by an Australian girl which goes to the tune of "Clementine":

Autumn

Willows swaying, gulls are flying,
See the water, still as glass;
Now it's autumn, it's so yellow,
Oh how quickly time does pass;
Golden sunshine, shining brightly,
See the clouds begin to form;
Slightly blowing is the soft breeze,
Rich and radiant autumn morn!
(P.R., Rosetta High School, Hobart, Australia)

As your pupils become more knowledgeable about sound, they should be able to write poetry more effectively and read it with fuller enjoyment.

Names Make Music

Sound is an ingredient of all poetry. Pupils should understand that this ingredient can occur in many forms, and that rhythm does not necessarily mean scansion or rhyme. Here is a form that will give your pupils practice with sound. Ask them to make a poem with the following first two lines:

>Names make music
>
>Canadian all, like

>_____, _____,
>
>_____, _____,
>
>_____, _____,
>
>_____, _____,

>Names make music
>
>Canadian all.

This is the framework of a sound poem in which the first two lines are followed by six or eight place names arranged so that they have rhythm and a sound pattern. The pupils must realize that the names they pick do not have to make any logical sense—they are not making an atlas—but they must make a sound sense.

Here are several pieces by young people in different countries:

>Names make music
>Hawaiian all, like
>Kapiolani, Kalakana,
>Iolani, Punahou,
>Ala moahana, kameameha,
>Kainlani, molokai,
>Names make music
>Hawaiian all.
>(S.M., Punahou School,
>Honolulu, Hawaii)

Names make music
Australian all, like
Oonadatta, Marble Bar,
Turramurra, Warrawee,
Coolongatta, Cabramatta,
Wiseman's Ferry, Coolgardie,
Names make music
Australian all.

(Ian Begbie, Cranbrook School,
Sydney, Australia)

Names make music
Kenyan all, like
Gedi, Mombassa,
Malindi, Nyeri,
Masai, Kikuyu,
Uhuru, harambee
Names make music
Kenyan all.

(Vijay Vithani, Jamhuri High
School, Nairobi, Kenya).

Once all your pupils have made one of these pieces, let them try to guess the country or locality described by their classmates. This exercise can serve as an interesting travelogue as well as a useful experience with sound.

Portrait of a Letter or Number

Letters and numbers have personalities much as people do. One can distinguish the difference in character between a *b* and an *s* as surely as one senses the distinction between a *3* and a *7*. Ask your pupils to concentrate on any letter or number, and to write a short two to four-line word portrait of it so as to bring out its distinctive features. They might like to focus on factors such as colour, shape, sound, or activity. A well-written portrait presents a type of character sketch of the letter or number, and makes it come alive for the reader. Try to guess the identity of these examples:

(i)

Tall, bold, tough, and strong,
Thick-shouldered, small-waisted,
Talkative.

(G. Plagerez, Phillips Exeter Academy, Exeter, U.S.A.)

Answer: T

(ii)

Almost a circle,
Half brother to the O;
It's always in circle,
But never in so.

(Peter Buckley, St. George's School, Vancouver, Canada)

Answer: C

(iii)

A busy hardworking number,
Used to make bets on the wheel;
An upside-down L tipping sideways
And followed by luck, people feel.

(Karin Boothroyd, Wagar High School, Montreal, Canada)

Answer: 7

(iv)

It's the strongest in the alphabet,
Female though it may be:
It's sterling silver inside out,
And gentle as the sea.

(Robert Parisi, Marist College, Perth, Australia)

Answer: S

(v)

Side by side they stand
Silent and sleek;
Identical lucky twins.

(R.S., Iolani School, Honolulu, Hawaii)

Answer: 11

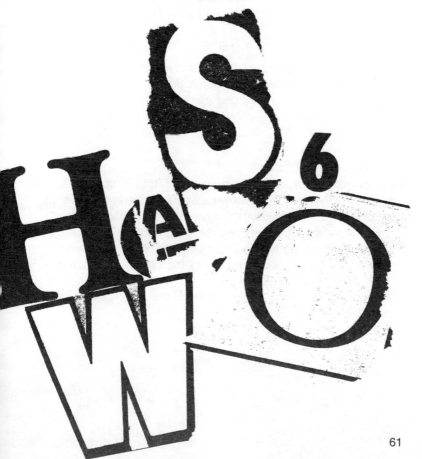

(vi)

Quite qualified for quacking
Quick followed by a quiescent sidekick,
Quiet
After its initial quip.
(T.L., Otter Valley High School, Brandon, U.S.A.)

Answer: Q

(vii)

A kind of blank, empty and straight,
Without anything, just depth,
Alone and silent.
(Jamie Reider, Jamhuri High School, Nairobi, Kenya)

Answer: O

Certain aspects of the portraits are worthy of note. In item (i), Guy has made effective use of alliterative sound devices in building his portrait of the letter *T*. The rhythm of item (iii), including the alternate line rhyme, is effective in describing the number *7*. In item (v), Robin has made a departure in describing the two cipher number *11*. In the final portrait, Jamie from East Africa has created a realistic characterization of the enigmatic *O*.

Your pupils might enjoy trying to identify their own pieces after they have made them in class.

Portrait From the Animal World

Young people everywhere seem to be captivated by the creatures of the animal kingdom. Capitalize on this interest by asking your pupils to make a portrait of an animal, insect, bird, or fish. Their piece should be no more than six lines long, and should contain sufficient detail to make it come alive.

We write best about what we know best. Hence a girl from Australia probably shouldn't try to write about a polar bear. Likewise, a Canadian boy shouldn't try to describe a kangaroo. If some of your pupils have never visited a zoo or game park, they might be best to start by writing about a domestic animal.

The Cat

Silky, slinky,
Slithering silently
Stepping softly,
Proud and dignified,
Black and beautiful.

(L. W., Dunton High School,
Montreal, Canada)

Giraffe

Tall, slender,
Gently moving,
Feeding on green acacia,*
Tawny-brown color
Grotesque in the glade.

(Zahida Qureshi, Jamhuri High School,
Nairobi, Kenya)

*Acacia is a type of shrub or tree
  yielding gum arabic.

*Yellowtail**

Mosaic of color and form,
Scintillating tail in the sunshine,
Playful and lively
Yellowtail.

(T. Manilius, Royal College,
Curepipe, Mauritius)

Featherling

There the featherling sits—
His head held high, his breast bulging;
There he sits enjoying the day,
Proud,
Proud of being a featherling.

(Ian Derrick, Peninsula School,
Mt. Eliza, Australia)

Eel

A slimish, underwater shocker,
A sliding, gliding paralizer:
Moves like a snake, a greenish snake.

(D.P., Punahou School, Honolulu, Hawaii)

*A type of tropical fish that abounds in the Indian Ocean off the beaches of
Mauritius.

65

King of the Basement

Our dog—he's black;
his name is Buck,
He's big—
He's king of the basement:
Our dog—he sleeps
and eats down there,
He's smart—
He's king of the basement:
But when, let up,
He causes a mess,
That's bad—
Back to the basement.

(R.B., Philaemon Wright High School, Hull, Canada)

The story behind the "Tortiss" poem is typical of many of the best pieces I have received on my travels. Danny Neate was in the lowest English set in his age group. In fact, I think there was even some question in the minds of the fathers at Downlands College whether they would bring Danny's set along to my writing session that day. It was a radiant afternoon as we sat outside on the oval overlooking the city of Toowoomba. I gave the boys no more than ten minutes in which to write. Danny's piece, reproduced here exactly as he wrote it, demonstrates that everyone has potential for writing, especially the supposedly less able.

Tortiss

Slowly trudgeing tirelessly,
no destination in mind;
Dordeling through a world
Of sleepy-eyed drowsieness;
His legs revolving in slowness;
The tortiss never gives up.

(Danny Neate, Downlands College,
Toowoomba, Australia)

Portrait of Yourself

During their school writing experiences, pupils are often asked to do character sketches, impressions of animals, and studies of people they know well. In this section, ask them to go a step further and try a self-portrait. Suggest that they concentrate not on physical features, as they would if attempting a mirror-image. Rather, let them compare themselves to any one of a number of things: the weather, a season of the year, a colour, a number, an object, or any item they feel is suitable.

This is no easy task, and the end product, if the pupils try the same exercise a number of times, will probably differ from day to day as their sense of the moment changes. "Know thyself" is a motto that applies for all seasons.

Myself

I am a play,
With all the laughter and tears
hidden backstage:
I am all the characters—
The heroine that I want to be,
the villain that I sometimes stoop to,
and the scenery,
the sun and the stars,
and the dingy slum buildings:
I am the brilliant scenes
and the clumsy, ashamed mistakes:
I am a play.

(L.F., Dunton High School, Montreal, Canada)

Myself

Always wondering who to be,
So easily changed by those you see.
(B.G., Bishop's College School,
Lennoxville, Canada)

68

Myself

**Myself, I'm like a telephone—
sometimes busy,
sometimes forgotten,
conveying the good news
and the bad,
and sometimes just gab:
I can be pink—
happy and cheery;
I can be black—
sad and mournful;
Although many look as I do,
I have a number which is all my own. . . .
Me, a telephone.**

*(M.M., Philaemon Wright High School,
Hull, Canada)*

Giggles

*Giggles,
and a sunset of brilliant orange;
a line without thought;
Flying a kite, and candy canes;
Ice cream delight,
A flash of stained-glass panes,
And then
blue-white snowflakes,
A morning in May
That's me.*
*(Diana A., Newton High School,
Boston, U.S.A.)*

Diana, one of the top young writers at Newton High School, has developed her self-portrait through the combination of a number of single images.

I Am Monarch of All I Survey*

Your pupils should be familiar with the expression "I am monarch of all I survey." Ask them to apply it to any creature of their choice—animal, fish, bird, or insect—and to write a poem from the inside-out, imagining that they *are* whatever creature they choose. They should try to put themselves into the mind and heart of their subject, and attempt to think and write as their creature would if it had a voice.

Remind your pupils that it is not only the largest and most powerful animals such as the lion, whale, or eagle, who have their kingdoms. Most creatures have distinct areas of influence even if these areas are as restricted as goldfish bowls or basement kennels.

Shark

Watchdog of the seas
Am I—
The most feared of fish:
No invader dares defy me,
For I am the monarch of the sea,
With gleaming eyes and razor teeth—
The Shark.

**(Z.B., Dunton High School,
Montreal, Canada)**

Goldfish

I live in my globe of glass,
With the weeds of home floating about me:
The gravel at the bottom
Glitters like gems from a pirate's chest:

---

* I am grateful for this idea to Miss Alice Shaw, an outstanding teacher of English in Montreal, Canada.

Make a Season

In many parts of the world, nature works dramatic changes through the four seasons. In Eastern Canada, for instance, we have green, hot days in summer giving way to flaming maple leaves in autumn. Winter wraps the landscape in snow before the new earth signals the spring.

Ask your pupils to write a five-line poem about their favourite season. Each line of the poem should portray one of the senses: sight, sound, smell, taste, and touch. Your pupils should try in each line to create images that are typical of that particular season.

Remember that seasons are reversed north and south of the equator. Winter in England, for instance, will be summer in New Zealand. Let your pupils guess these seasons:

A flash of crackling colours;
The snap of the cold clean air;
The smell of ten thousand burning leaves;
The honking of geese flying south;
Roast pork with home-made apple sauce;
Autumn.

(Peter Hickey, Gatineau Elementary School,
Gatineau, Canada)

Sticky, icy windows;
Nose blocked up;
Frost on dying paddocks;
Cattle snorting;
Hot cocoa in the early morning;
Winter.

(C. Fogarty, Downlands College,
Toowoomba, Australia)

I see the heat rising from a melting road;
I hear the still silence;
I feel the sweat pouring out of me;
I smell the fumes in the dead air;
I taste cool water on my tongue;
Summer.
(Ian Shillington, St. Ignatius College,
Sydney, Australia)

Leaping puddles splashing;
The scent of birth;
Green buds;
Sweet cool sap, sipped from a bucket;
Squish-
Spring.

(Cindy Russell, Forest Dale School,
Brandon, U.S.A.)

Brandon is a quiet town almost lost in the rolling, tree-covered hills of rural Vermont. Cindy lives there and has observed her surroundings well. She speaks of the maple sap which is tapped each spring in shiny buckets. She describes the mud and wetness caused by the melting snow—"squish." Her poem works because she has observed and appreciated her distinctive part of the world.

Subject at Different Times

The same subject can have a completely different appearance and character at different times of the year. Consider the Canadian maple tree for example. In the summer it stands full and stately, clothed in dark green. In the autumn it turns all colours—orange, red, yellow—and makes hillsides blaze with its fire. In winter it shivers, a bare skeleton against snow and sky. In spring it is covered with the buds of new birth. The very same maple tree has different characteristics in each of the four seasons; thus presenting a kaleidoscope of sights and moods throughout the year.

Ask your pupils to make a poem about a similar subject; perhaps a river, park bench, city square, window pane, dirt road, or flower pot. Let them write a short piece—three or four lines long—describing the subject in each of the four seasons.

Seasons *River*

Summer *Ripple, ripple,*
Downhill water flows,
Smashing against rocks,
Spraying.

Autumn *Choke,*
River clogged with leaves,
Trying to grasp a breath,
Before it sinks beneath.

Winter *Gurgle, gurgle,*
River made of ice,
Last resort,
Sun beaming bright.

Spring *Water from all over,*
Trying to snatch a place,
Overloaded river,
Flood.

(S. W., Philaemon Wright High School, Hull, Canada)

Garden

Now it's winter
And I'm forgotten
Snow, deep snow
Covers this garden

Spring roars in,
And I'm alive again;
Seeds and weeds
Keep me company.

Hot sunny days,
Ripe tomatoes,
Big brown potatoes
I like summer best.

Autumn is scary;
Bugs crawl through me;
Feet tramp on me;
Hands grab at me.

(John G., Philaemon Wright High School,
Hull, Canada)

John has made his piece in the first person, an approach which gives warmth to his writing.

Window Pane

Winter	Frost plays its game of patterns Long, spidery, Thick or dense.
Spring	Drop races drop, Speeding down The polished surface.
Summer	Hot, humid rays Steam The pane.
Autumn	Window, barrier to autumn cold Keeps in heat, But tells no tale of what's outside.

(A.S., Westmount High School,
Montreal, Canada)

Times of the Day

As an extension of this idea, ask your pupils to write about the same subject at three or four different times of the day. Many topics lend themselves to this treatment: school, a subway station, a barnyard, a campsite, shadows from a tree. By becoming conscious of differing moods and appearances through closer observation, pupils will gain a fuller appreciation of life around them.

Main Street

8 A.M. *Overflowing with traffic,*
All rushing for a place,
Suffocating the street.

11 A.M. *Running smoothly;*
No pushing
Mid-day flow.

1 A.M. *No one here now,*
Quiet, deserted:
Cats prowl.

(R.H., Marymount High School, Montreal, Canada)

Transformation

Sometimes if you look carefully and use your imagination, you can see things changing before your eyes. Consider cloud formations on a windy day, for instance. They shift and move, and assume different shapes. They are transformed many times as you watch them.

Ask your pupils to think of a subject that changes, like a sunrise, a flower opening, smoke from a chimney. They should then write a poem tracing the transformations.

Peter Jones is ten years old, and goes to Park School in Brandon, Manitoba. In this poem he outlines the changes that he imagined as he watched a Canadian prairie sunset:*

In the sunset
You might see
Little old women
Drinking tea.

Maybe you see,
A beautiful tree,
As in the autumn
With colourful leaves.

But what I see
Is a tropical island;
The colours are like parrots' feathers,
And crabs are crawling in the sun.

But before my eyes it changes;
And then I see a bullfight
With the cape flashing in the sun;
At the other end I see dirt flying,
And then the scene dies.

*This poem, "Sunset," is discussed on p. 144.

Here are two other pieces done by young writers on subjects that change:

Cloud

Water vapour supported by the wind?
No, it's a tired old face
That twists and turns, and
Becomes a camel that loses its hump,
And as a horse, rides over the horizon.

(W.B., Brandon Collegiate Institute,
Brandon, Canada)

Blue-Tailed Guppy

Slowly, silently,
As my fish swims across the tank,
I think of a ballerina dancing on the stage—
So delicate.

(D.T., Santa Sabena Convent, Sydney, Australia)

Moment of Creation

Everything in the world around us comes into being at some specific point in time; it has its moment of creation. This moment might be a birth in the animal or human sense, or it might be the combination of various creative processes as is the case with an artist's picture or in the assembly of a watch.

Ask your pupils to think about the moment of creation. Suggest that they write a short poem about this moment, using as their topic any subject that captures their interest—perhaps a building, a sculpture, an animal, an idea. Read them several of these examples to trigger their thoughts:

Calf

Coming out of its mother
All slimy
Completely lifeless,
It's dead;
no—
Look, it's breathing;
It moves its head and tongue
It staggers,
Stands on four feet—
A new life.

(Ken B., Pittwater House Grammar School, Collaroy, Australia)

Ken arrived late at school on the day he wrote this poem. He told me that he had been up all night helping his dad deliver a calf on their Australian outback property. It had been an unforgettable experience.

Popcorn

Nestled, labouring,
Tapping sightlessly
Against a steel cell;
Rolling, twirling,
Exploding into white snow crystals—
Popcorn.

(Beth Thompson, Scotch College,
Adelaide, Australia)

Dawn

First the whiteness that makes the black tree blacker:
Then the cool red glow behind the distant hills;
Then the brightness and the pale rays sweeping;
Then the dawn.

(Russ Schneider, Marcellin College, Melbourne, Australia)

Clown

A man, tired and old,
Sits before a mirror:
He paints a face,
smeared with white;
He applies a nose,
that is red and cheery;
Then adds a smile
to prove he's happy:
A clown.

(Sherry Russell,
Otter Valley High School,
Brandon, U.S.A.)

79

Changing Environment

All things change over time. In recent years, the pace of industrial development has brought dramatic alterations to the face of the globe. Not all these changes have been good.

Young people around the world have been captivated by the pollution-ecology theme. Ask them to write a short piece— something under eight lines long— in which they describe any aspect of our wasting environment. Here are a few examples:

Bay

A bay used to be here,
With cedars and pines,
In their natural state,
By this sandy shore;
But now it's abused;
The cedars lie hewn;
The sand is cement;
The bay is no more.

(H.A., Sir Winston Churchill High School, Montreal, Canada)

More

The air was clean, until man wanted more;
The water was lively, until man needed more;
The earth was quiet until man built machines.

(S.C., Dunton High School, Montreal, Canada)

Our Land

Look at our soil;
Look at our trees;
The open sea and plains,
Let us not waste our land.

(Shee Mazoa, Jamhuri High School, Nairobi, Kenya)

Shee is a Swahili boy who lives in East Africa. Even in his country, famed for its beauty and wildlife, man is destroying nature.

I'm Growing Old

A logical extension of the pollution theme is the thought that all things decay as they get older. Objects or people, once proud and at the height of their powers, fall into disuse or fade off the stage. Ask your pupils to think of a subject for which this situation holds true—a sports car, a party dress, a soft drink can, a favourite toy, a politican—and to write about its passing in ten lines or less.

Horse

Once proud, with a mane like fire,
He could run like the wind—
For as long as he wanted:
Now a broken-down nag—
His mane like straw,
His legs like boards,
He waits in his stall,
Unneeded.

(E.C., Monklands High School,
Montreal, Canada)

Flowers

In a vase lies the trash,
Old, brown, and dead:
Yesterday they were flowers,
Colourful and dancing.

(S.P., Sydney Grammar School,
Sydney, Australia)

Old Man

Old and bent,
Tired and gray,
He shuffles along, cane in hand:
He opens the door,
And sits in the chair—
Alone:
Today is his birthday.

(Michael R., Wagar High School, Montreal, Canada)

Wagar High School in Montreal is located directly opposite the Griffith McConnell Home for Senior Citizens. Michael, who wrote this piece above, noticed one particular old man and discovered his story. He captures its poignancy in his poem.

Doll

She sits on a shelf,
Pushed to the back,
Hidden by records,
and pictures of boyfriends:
She used to be the favourite,
But now she sits on a shelf—
Pushed to the back.

(H.B., Lachine High School,
Montreal, Canada)

Progressive Narrative

The narrative exercises a form of control over any writing. It presents an ordered sequence of events, a progressive development. Ask your pupils to write a narrative poem which evolves logically both in time and incident.

Here is a poem by a young Hawaiian girl. She eventually made it into a small book in which each line appeared on a different page—twelve in all—with an accompanying illustration for each. Your pupils might like to experiment with this idea.

*Happiness**

When God was still experimenting,
Man was never uncomfortable,
And he had no worrysome responsibilities:
But this life without error was monotonous;
So God thought about this problem for awhile,
And finally decided to give man
Danger,
Pain,
And fear.
The escape from these troubles
Made ordinary things seem nicer.
Man was finally happy.

(G.L., Punahou School, Honolulu, Hawaii)

An extension of the narrative poem can often be achieved in the parody. Young people seem to enjoy doing humourous take-offs on all sorts of topics. Suggest to your pupils that they make a

*This poem is mentioned on p. 139.

parody which has a set rhythm; it rhymes and scans. As an illustration, read them this piece which is written in rhyme couplets and iambic tetrameter:

The Ballad of Lassie, The Vanquisher*

And in Suburbia wood one day,
dog Lassie and boy Tim did play:
And they had fun between the woods,
As every boy and dog well should.

But look, tube fan, in yonder grass,
There lurks the deadly snake, alas!
And there is close-up-shot, fangs beg,
For Timmy's prepubescent leg.

O what can save poor Timmy's life?
And nowhere is a gun, a knife;
And you, the viewer, sweats but knows,
That Lassie vanquishes her foes.

In colour, snake's head rises high:
Will Lassie pass and let it lie?
She barks a warning; Timmy knows,
That Lassie vanquishes her foes.

Her head held high, she circles round,
In one big technicolored bound,
She beats the snake at his own game,
And goes for Timmy's Throat, for shame!

(Bill Parke, Phillips Exeter Academy, Exeter, U.S.A.)†

*Certainly Lassie and Tim are no strangers to children the world over. Who hasn't at one time or another watched the courageous collie Lassie save her master Timmy from all sorts of danger 24 hours a day.

†Bill wrote this piece when he was fifteen years old. He later went on to become editor of *The Exonian*, the oldest prep school newspaper in America—and to a distinguished writing career at Stanford University.

Specific Triggers

Prepare in prose the outline of a specific situation for your pupils. Describe this situation to them in some detail, thus providing them with a trigger for their thought. Then ask them to write a poem about whatever the trigger has suggested to them. Here are a number of ideas to supplement your own:

Gulls

Imagine that you are sitting on the beach watching a number of gulls circling in the air. At one moment they hover, poised above the waves. At another, they find a thermal, and wheel on it in great circles high in the sky. They are always in motion—graceful, restless.

Gulls

Gulls
Moving in the air,
Sweeping,
Gliding,
Rising higher,
higher,
Gracefully they fly.
(B.P., Belmont Hill School,
Boston, U.S.A.)

Gulls

A circle of gulls,
Thermalling—
Specks of white
Spiralling higher, higher,
Freedom searchers,
Riding the breeze.
(D.M., Phillips Exeter Academy,
Exeter, U.S.A.)

Subway Station

Imagine that you are standing on the platform of a crowded subway station at rush hour. You are surrounded by a confusion of sights and sounds. Suddenly there is a blur of lights and flashing steel; a subway express bursts from the dark cavern at the end of the platform and roars through the station. It doesn't stop.

Underwater Pool

Imagine that you are equipped with skin-diving gear and that you are exploring an underwater pool. Around you is a profusion of exotic fish, coral outcrops, strange beds of weeds, and other undersea wonders. Describe anything you observe.

Seaweed

**Slithering and reaching,
Flowing mysteriously,
Fanning about crazily —
Seaweed.**

(R.M., Punahou School, Honolulu, Hawaii)

The Bottom

Bubbles
White and silver,
Dance to the surface:
Green strands of life wave;
Rocks, jagged and smooth,
Shield a moray eel
And fish with colours of the spectrum.

(Andrew Pugh, Northmount High School, Montreal, Canada)

Campfire

Imagine that you have just cooked your own supper outside. Darkness has fallen, and you are sitting beside the embers of your campfire. Brightly coloured sparks drift into the air, and a red glow touches the bushes and stones nearby. A coyote calls.

City at Night

Imagine that you are standing high on some vantage point, looking down on the city at night. Below you are lights in a hundred patterns. Some are moving like ants with headlamps; others are forming brilliant neon clusters. Tall buildings look like Christmas trees trimmed with silver ornaments.

Make up a number of similar triggers of your own that might interest your pupils. Something specific as a start often sparks a response in young writers whose powers of observation are not yet highly developed.

Your Mind Can Fly

The mind is a marvellous instrument. It can carry you to far-away places as you sit in a room. Your imagination can take you ahead in time while your memory can take you back. Try these two suggestions:

My Mind Is Like a Jet Plane

Point out to your pupils that while their bodies shackle them to one place, their minds can travel anywhere, and as quickly as the speed of thought: "Four walls do not a prison make, nor iron bars a cage." Propose the fact that they can circle the globe in a few seconds in their minds. Then ask them to write a poem about any aspect of the idea that intrigues them.

I Travel

Through endless time I sit in class,
My body chained beneath me:
I open my mind,
Turn the lock on the door,
And fly the countryside:
I soar above continents,
And through woods to the sea—
What do I care?
There's nothing but air—
Not even the bell can stop me.

(S.F., Wagar High School, Montreal, Canada)

Skiing

Skiing up a slope,
Tumbling through powder,
Flying over jumps,
Falling around moguls—
All these I accomplish
at my wooden desk
For my body is a cage,
But my mind is a plane.

(D.A., Monklands High School,
Montreal, Canada)

Memory—Let It Fly

Remind your pupils that even on the darkest days the memory can serve to bring back the sunshine. It can recreate experiences, adventures, thrills, and bring yesterday into today. Let your pupils use this idea as a springboard to make up poems of their own.

Squirrel

Dash across the lawn
Squirrel of gray,
Running through my mind,
On a winter day.

(T.B., St. Johnsbury Academy,
St. Johnsbury, U.S.A.)

Sunshine

My mind is flooded
with a thousand memories
of sunshine days, and walks with my dog
as he was dying:
And now I remember,
The sun shone that day too.

(Brenda Watson, Lyndon Institute,
Lyndonville, U.S.A.)

Brenda told me that the loss of her dog was the greatest sorrow in her life until then. Even sadness on the day of his death, however, did not blind her to the life-giving beauty of the rays of the sun.

These Walls Could Tell Some Stories

Not long ago I was doing some writing amid the ruins of an old fort on Botany Bay in Sydney, Australia. It was a sparkling day, the two hundredth anniversary of the discovery of Australia. In less than three hours I was to see the royal yacht Britannia sail through the Heads so that the Queen could watch a re-enactment of Captain Cook's first landing at this place.

Two elderly men entered the circular blockhouse area where I was sitting. At one time, long ago, it had been used as a prison for convicts. The men looked at the massive walls. They studied the heavy iron rings in the masonry, and the chains on the floor. Then one turned to the other and said: "These walls could tell some stories."

My own mind travelled back through time to harsher days, and the room came alive in my imagination.

Ask your pupils to write about any situation which may have given them a similar feeling. Obviously their situation need not be an ancient fortress. It might be their own school classroom as they think back to generations of former pupils, or a book, or a favourite quiet place. Whatever the circumstances, let them use as their theme the thought in the statement by the old gentleman: "These walls could tell some stories."

The Anchor

This rusty anchor
At the bottom of the sea —
What stories it could tell.

Of green lands, blue seas,
Of strange people and emptiness —
What stories it could tell.

Of wrecked ships and fleeing convicts,
Of water lapping 'round the hull —
What stories it could tell.

This rusty anchor,
At the bottom of the sea —
What stories it could tell.

(Paula S., Santa Sabena Convent, Sydney, Australia)

At the start of the class in which the above piece was written, I had shown the girls a sea shell heavily stained with the rust of an anchor. Paula thought about it, and then wrote her poem "The Anchor."

Walls have infinite settings, as the next two poems reveal.

Walls of S.I.C.*

I look at the walls of S.I.C.
What stories they relate to me;
Stories of classes, exams and fun;
Stories of the lives of everyone;
Tales of teachers, some good,
Some bad.
Tales of rabblers,† and the fun they had;
What stories these walls relate to me,
These precious walls of S.I.C.

*S.I.C. is the abbreviation for St. Ignatius College, Riverview, in Sydney, Australia.
† "Rabbler" is an Australian slang term for a troublesome pupil, an active mischief-maker.

Book

Between the covers,
A new world of mystery, romance, action,
Pleasure for all;
Time has no meaning—
A hundred years into the future—
All in a second;
The key to imagination
Kings, heroes, pirates—they are real, alive,
The pages are alive.
(D.B., St. George's School, Montreal, Canada)

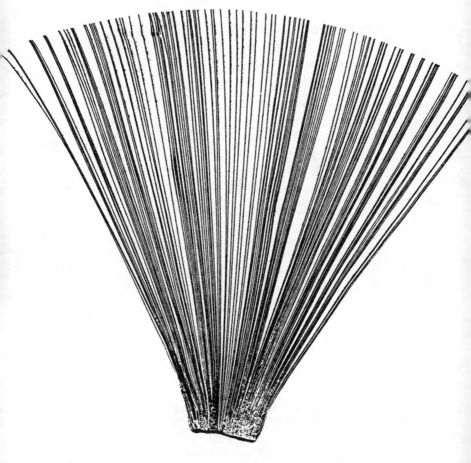

Contrasts

We are confronted by contrasts on all sides—night, day; heat, cold; winter, summer; youth and age. Contrasts are everywhere: in colours, speeds, shades of meaning.

Ask your pupils to write about any contrast that interests them. Let them make a short poem—not more than five lines long—on each side of the contrast of their choice. In doing so they should try to bring distinctive features to life, and attempt to capture the spirit of their subject.

Night and Day

Night is darkness,
Silence,
A piece of velvet;
A black book closing its covers.

Day is noise,
Crowded sidewalks,
Honking horns,
Brass-button sun warming everything.

(T.L., Westmount High School, Montreal, Canada)

Wood/Plastic*

Wood, soft,
Rubbed down by a thousand hands
To a rich red-brown.

Plastic, sharp,
A perfect shape,
A year old
And still 16 1/7 millimeters long.

(A.C., Putney High School, Putney, U.S.A.)

* See p. 138 for a discussion of this poem.

Fire/Water

Fire,
Thriving on things that water grows;
Water,
Killing fire wherever it goes.
(J.M., St. George's School, Montreal, Canada)

City Kid/Country Kid

A city kid has soul,
Dancing on the dirty steps,
"Kool and the Gang" blaring away,
A city kid has rock and roll.

A country kid has silence,
Trudging through new-fallen snow,
Flakes stinging his face,
A country kid has soul too.

(Tim Daly, Putney School, Putney, U.S.A.)

Each of these pieces captures, in its own way, the spirit of its subject. I think the final image of the first piece—"brass-button sun warming everything"—is particularly successful. The staccato rhythm in the second part of "Wood/Plastic" is also effective as is the substance and insight of "City Kid/Country Kid." Tim Daly lives in the heart of New York City and boards at Putney School in rural Vermont. He has experienced both sides of the life about which he writes.

Time and Motion Contrasts

Contrast in Time

Read your pupils this poem by Langston Hughes, an outstanding twentieth century black writer:

City: San Francisco

In the morning, the city
Spreads its wings,
Making a song
In stone that sings.

In the evening, the city
Goes to bed,
Hanging lights
About its head.

Anyone who knows San Francisco should appreciate this word portrait. Hughes presents a contrast in his two verses between the start and the end of the day; this is contrast in time. Notice that the second and fourth lines of each verse rhyme, thus providing a unifying thread through sound.

Ask you pupils to make a similar two-verse poem in which they present some contrast in time.

Life Span

In youth, a man
With thoughts of life,
Sees only joy
And never strife.

In age a man
With thoughts of rest,
Remembers grief—
Forgets the best.

(J.B., York House School,
Vancouver, Canada)

The Sky

At dawn, the sky
In pink array,
Awaits the birth
Of an unborn day.

At dusk the sky
In golden tone
Withdraws its light,
Leaving night alone.

(Mary Mallon, Lyndon Institute,
Lyndonville, U.S.A.)

Mary has always been near the top of her class in English, probably because she is observant. She lives in the peaceful town of Lyndonville in northern Vermont, an area noted for its colours, particularly its autumn foliage, its sunrises, and sunsets.

Contrast in Motion

As an extension of the above idea, ask your pupils to think of some contrast in motion. To start off read them Alfred, Lord Tennyson's poem "The Eagle":

He clasps the crag with crooked hands;
Close to the sun in lonely lands;
Ringed with the azure world, he stands.

The wrinkled sea beneath him crawls;
He watches from his mountain walls;
And like a thunderbolt, he falls.

The first of these two 3-line stanzas is basically a description of the eagle on his perch. It is static. The second stanza conveys action as the eagle plummets onto his prey. Ask your pupils to compose a similar two-stanza poem. Their piece should contain some definite rhyme scheme, though not necessarily the same one as Tennyson's, in which they present an at-rest/in-motion contrast between their stanzas.

Here are two very graphic examples of this mode:

City

City-sleeping,
Night-steeping,
Silence-keeping avenues.

Day-glaring,
Horns-blaring,
No-one caring, ugly views.

(Debbie Earl, West Hill High School,
Montreal, Canada)

Wind

Light breeze swinging,
Red leaves singing,
Summer phrases, soft and warm.

Torrents stinging,
Cold winds flinging,
Sodden leaves throughout the storm.

(H.H., Dunton High School, Montreal, Canada)

Rhyme Couplets

The aborigines were the earliest inhabitants of the continent of Australia. Their present-day descendants are still fighting for equality of opportunity in their own country. One of their spokeswomen is Kath Walker, who has written the following poem:

Aboriginal Charter of Rights

We want hope, not racialism;
Brotherhood, not ostracism;
Black advance, not white ascendance;
Make us equals, not dependants;
We need help, not exploitation;
We want freedom, not frustration;
Must we native Old Australians,
In our own land rank as aliens?
Banish bans, and conquer caste;
Then we'll win our own at last.

Pupils will notice that this piece is composed of a series of rhyme couplets and that within each line there is a type of contrast: "We want hope, not racialism." Ask them to follow this model in making a poem of their own on any issue about which they feel strongly.

Why do we?

Why do we hate, if loving is better?
Why do we fight, when agreeing is wiser?
Why do we destroy, if creation is needed?
Why do we laugh, when tears go unheeded?
(J.F., Wagar High School, Montreal, Canada)

The following poem, written by a young English-speaking pupil, strikes at the heart of Canada's language and cultural problem:

Why Not Both Languages?

We want our language, not that of the majority;
They want their language, not that of the minority;
Why not both languages, not just one?
Then all could communicate, not just some.

(P.H., Monklands High School, Montreal, Canada)

Don't Tie Our Hands

Let us be free, not totally directed;
Choosing our way, not having it selected;
Let us discover, not always be told;
Form our own ideas, not the one's we've been sold;
We need suggestions not rigid commands;
Give us some guidance, but don't tie our hands.

(Liz Hogg, Montreal West High School, Montreal, Canada)

Liz makes a useful statement here, one that is both strong yet moderate. She has expressed much of what is positive in the thinking of today's young people.

Prose-Poetry Combinations

One of the aims of the approach suggested in this book is practice in the use of words. The more forms young writers can try, the wider will be their experience.

Ask your pupils to write a prose piece on any subject that interests them, and then to treat the same subject poetically. Don't get involved here in technicalities of definition: "What *is* poetry anyway?" It might be worth suggesting, however, that poetry is usually a more concise form of expression than prose; hence the poetry piece will probably have fewer words than the prose. Also it probably has a rhythm that may be lacking in prose, although it certainly need not rhyme.

As an illustration of this prose-poetry combination read your pupils the following pieces written by a seventeen-year-old boy in Papua New Guinea. They tell of a walk he took in the jungle near his home in the Garoka highlands. You might be interested to know that English is this young man's third language. I met him when he was just starting a course in teacher training.

DAWN TRIP
As the day began to break, we set off on our journey. Outside the jungle it was bright and hot, but inside it was dark and cool as we began to be attacked by thousands of mosquitoes. They came from every direction, and landed on us from head to toe. Regardless of what we did, we were unable to drive them away. (63 words)

Walking and running we entered the forest,
Our first enemy met us —
Mosquitoes:
From our heads to our feet,
In thousands they attacked us —
In thousands they came.

  (28 words)

(G.M., Garoka Teacher's College, Garoka, Papua New Guinea)

Your pupils will notice that the poetry version above is less than half as long as the prose. They should also notice that in the poetry, the writer is able to give prominence to the word "mosquitoes," by having it stand on a line of its own.

Prose-Telegram

Here is another exercise which should serve as a link with your regular work in composition or language arts. Ask your pupils again to write a short prose passage on any subject of interest to them. Then let them imagine that they are sending a telegram to a friend who is far-away. In this telegram, which is to cost them ten cents a word, they are to transmit the essence of their prose message by omitting conjunctions, pronouns, and other insignificant words. They should try to trim the telegram to the bone without leaving out any important details. Here is a piece of prose written by a girl in Tasmania, Australia. She reduced it to three words for her telegram. Let your pupils guess what the three words are!

> The world spun. I was swallowed by the liquid blue. Movement became easy as I lay suspended on my back. Crystal spheres danced up past my eyes and burst out of the blue, breaking the solid silver ceiling and spreading ripples across the surface above.
> (45 words)

Telegram:
WENT SCUBA DIVING
(Jane H., Friends School, Hobart, Australia)

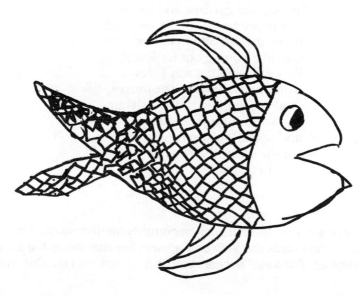

Poetry and Pop Songs

Close links have always existed between poetry and music. The Psalms in the Bible are essentially poems set to music. Wandering minstrels in the Middle Ages wrote pieces to be accompanied by the lute and the lyre. Many of today's pop stars—Bob Dylan, Leonard Cohen, John Lennon, Cat Stevens, and others—sing adaptations of poems.

Ask your pupils to bring the words of a number of their favourite record hits to school. Study them with your class, and help your pupils to see that many lyrics are twentieth century poems, and the singers, the minstrels of today.

As an example, look at the images in the last stanza of "Suzanne Takes You Down" by Montreal poet and folksinger Leonard Cohen:

Now Suzanne takes your hand
and she leads you to the river;
she is wearing rags and feathers
from Salvation Army counters.
And the sun pours down like honey
on our lady of the harbour
as she shows you where to look
among the garbage and the flowers.
There are heroes in the seaweed,
there are children in the morning;
they are leaning out for love,
they will lean that way forever
while Suzanne holds the mirror.
And you want to travel with her
and you want to travel blind
and you know you can trust her
for she's touched your perfect body
with her mind.

A piece such as this offers rich opportunity for discussion. It is interesting to note that with only a few minor alterations, the same version of "Suzanne" appears both in a collection of Mr. Cohen's poetry as well as on one of his record albums. What features of this poem-song make it so readily transferable from one medium to the other? Observe how the poet transforms such uninviting objects as rags and garbage into symbols of beauty. Let your pupils discuss the gentle, dreamlike mood of the piece and its highly visual quality. How do they think he achieved these effects? By a careful reading of the words members of your class should be able to establish a character portrait of the narrator as well as of "Suzanne."

Next your pupils might enjoy trying to create similar poem-songs of their own. If any of them can provide musical accompaniment, encourage them to do so.

Here is one example of a pupil making a link between poetry and music. Richard Cleaver, a seventeen-year-old boy at Phillips Exeter Academy, lives beside the sea, and has always been fascinated by it. He wrote the following sonnet after listening a number of times to the music of "Ebb Tide."

Wave

My birth is in the mountains and I die
On the sea-strand. Eternally reborn
And ever-dying mingling am I
In other waves, and yet I do not mourn
My endless cycle. I let it rise and fall
Wreathing my brow with darts and glints of light
Stolen from the sun and greeting all
By whom I pass with song by day and night:
By day and night embracing as I go,
All those who dwell within my bosom and
Caress those who live on my banks. Below
I run to the sea, and die upon the sand,
Yet I am not dead, for above I spring
Again, and downward all my greetings bring.

(Richard Cleaver, Phillips Exeter Academy, Exeter, U.S.A.)

Homer Hogan and Ken Weber have made a successful attempt to link pop music and poetry in their book *Poetry of Relevance* (Methuen). Try to do something similar in your own classroom.

What Interests You Most?

Everyone has particular interests, hobbies, sports, leisure time activities, and so on. Ask your pupils to think about something that genuinely interests them. Let them make a poem about it in which one of their aims is to try to share their enthusiasm with others.

Encourage your pupils to consider a wide range of topics. Any interest will do. Above all, it should be personal. They will write with more impact about things they know from direct experience.

Here are a few pieces as a start:

Fishing

We took off,
The engine roared,
The foam left behind
We reached our destination:
I dropped my line;
It tugged;
I tugged;
Up came a wonderful
Shiny, slithery, wriggly snapper.

(Warren Foster, Marist College,
Perth, Australia)

Art

Art is my favourite:
Painting, and imaging strange things:
Sketching, and tracing, and colouring in—
Taking my mind away.

(Lee Schneider, Norwood High School, Adelaide, Australia)

104

Collage of Emotions

Each day we are subject to a range of emotions: fear, anger, like, dislike, amusement, happiness, sorrow, and so on. The combination of these emotions produces our mood of any given moment.

Ask your pupils to create a word portrait of themselves by combining a number of emotions. If your pupils know one another well, you might read out a number of their collages, without mentioning any names, and then ask the others to try to identify the author.

I like fires on cold winter nights,
*   and popcorn smothered in hot butter;*
I dislike cold, tiled floors in the morning,
*   and people who put others down because of their colour.*

I feel depressed when I think of those
*   fighting the war,*
And I pity those who are alone:
I feel relieved when I pass my tests,
*   and happy when the first snow comes:*
I admire those who give their best to their country:
I fear violence and hatred.

(S.M., Riverdale High School, Montreal, Canada)

With further reworking, the rhythm of the above piece could be tightened and improved. Such a task might prove a useful exercise for your class.

> I like life, nature, and ginger beer:
> I dislike Coke, and flashy Detroit cars;
> I fear the future and what lies ahead;
> I pity those who go nine to five,
>   and admire those striving hard for a goal.
> (D.G., Belmont Hill School, Boston, U.S.A.)

I like the anticipation of something to come,
The co-ordination and finesse of a sport well done,
The Simon and Garfunkles—and all that, and some.

I feel depressed when there seems no point at all,
or nostalgic when another summer turns to fall,
or sad when someone tries to run who can't even crawl.

When I feel fear, I mostly fear fear;
and I'm scared when a nightmare is too clear;
And I am worried by things I cannot hear.

(C.S., Crown Woods Comprehensive School,
London, England)

A sincerely written collage gives an insight into the personality of the young person who has created it. Each of the three writers above is a distinctive individual, one we know better after sharing his/her thoughts.

Adventure

Adventure, by its definition, suggests a departure from the everyday, an experience out of the ordinary. At the time it is actually taking place, the adventure is often difficult, demanding, even unpleasant. In retrospect, however, it frequently seems to produce some of the high moments from which character is shaped.

Most young people like and seek adventure of all kinds. Ask your pupils to write about any adventure that they have experienced. They should choose a situation that involves some hardship either physical, mental, or spiritual. It should be real to them. Do you remember Sir Ernest Shackleton's famous advertisement from the 1906 London *Times:* "Men wanted for hazardous journey: small wages, bitter cold, long months of complete darkness, constant danger, safe return doubtful; honour and recognition in case of success"?

This section offers scope to young writers. It also gives you, the teacher, an opportunity to suggest any number of adventures from literature as a type of introduction to the writing. The twentieth century in particular has produced a succession of explorers and adventurers to the polar regions, up the highest mountains, under water, into outer space. Range freely over them all.

Here is a poem by a Queensland girl as a start:

Now

Probe,
Let you mind run wild;
Feel,
Explore what you see;
Live,
Discover what you can;
Now.

(Kathy Gleeson, Downlands College,
Toowoomba, Australia)

The Ulysses Factor

The legendary Greek hero Ulysses is famed for his determination and irrepressible will. He was filled with a thirst for adventure that prompted him to look for the unusual and to refuse to accept defeat. He was always seeking the next horizon.

Sir Winston Churchill was charged with this same spirit. The words of his final public speech delivered to the boys of Harrow School probably best capture the spirit of the man, and indeed of the Ulysses factor itself: "Never give up; never, never."

Ask your pupils to take as their theme the Ulysses factor, and to write a short poem about any aspect of it they want. Their piece should be personal if possible.

Go on

Go on,
Push yourself—
Push yourself to fame:
Walk through cannibal country,
Or just learn to swim;
Go on;
Push yourself.

**(P.B., Illminster Grammar School,
Somerset, England)**

Do it

Do it;
Make it better;
Fail;
Try again;
Reach:
Do it.

(J.B., St. George's School,
Vancouver, Canada)

Ambition

Climb the highest mountain;
Swim the largest River;
Run your longest mile;
Fight your strongest enemy;
Never give up.

**(M.W., West Hill High School,
Montreal, Canada)**

The Impossible

Tangle yourself
In unknown positions;
Feel the impossible;
Think the impossible;
Do the impossible.

(P.B., Punahou School,
Honolulu, Hawaii)

Yes

No hope:
You may as well give up:
When somebody says
'Yes'
Three letters are a miracle.

(John Deller, St. John's School,
Selkirk, Canada)

The setting for this final poem is the annual 50-mile snowshoe race held by the boys of St. John's School on the windswept prairies of Western Canada. John Deller's team had all but given up hope of completing the course. The captain asked his teammates if they felt they could face the last ten miles of darkness and sub-zero temperatures. One of the boys gave an emphatic yes. His spirit lifted the others to their goal, and a poem was born.

The Greatest Word in the World

Ask your pupils to pick from the entire scope of the English language a single word. This word must be the one which to them is the most significant, the most important, the most powerful, the most influential—the greatest word of them all.

In establishing the frame of reference, make your definition purposely broad. Pupils must realize that they are looking for a far-reaching word, and that it may have either a negative or a positive connotation. For example, they might want to chose the word *hate* if they feel its power is the most significant in the world today. Or if they wish to propose a proper noun, they might as readily nominate *Hitler* as *Churchill*.

Your pupils should realize that there is no "right answer" to this suggestion. The only right answer is their own carefully considered choice. The exercise might even lead to some formal debating with each pupil defending his/her own word. Within any class a wide range of choice is likely to arise.

Here are some sample words:

life	freedom	trust
power	hate	brotherhood
happiness	knowledge	family
poverty	friendship	no
unity	justice	giving
jealousy	understanding	acceptance
money	war	beauty
peace	patience	pride
God	love	evil
death	fear	hope
search	friends	harmony
future	help	strength
yes	people	belief
consideration	tolerance	

After all the pupils have chosen their words, they should build short poems around their selections. The pieces can take any form; they might be a definition or a pupil's reaction to the word or how the pupil feels his/her word influences others.

Here are a few examples:

Love

There is one lifeline
spanning the open sea,
To which have clung desperately
The people of all the centuries;
So thin, so easy to be cut;
Many have drowned when it broke for them,
Because no one has learned to swim without it.

(Bill Snow, Phillips Exeter Academy, Exeter, U.S.A.)

Home

A welcoming smile,
Open arms,
A giving,
A warm closeness,
Home.

(T.P., University of Toronto School,
Toronto, Canada)

Sacrifice

One of us had to wait;
Would it be him or me?
Who would go first?
I let him go.

(E.L., The King's School,
Parramatta, Australia)

Celebration

In most countries, special occasions are marked by celebrations. Ask your pupils to think about one such occasion—whether it be firecracker night, Anzac Day, a luau, or whatever—and to describe it in a poem of not more than eight lines in length. In order to make the occasion come alive, they should try to concentrate on distinctive details such as sights, sounds, and happenings.

Here are some examples with a brief explanation about each:

Rock Concert

Several times a year a rock concert is held inside the crater of Diamond Head, an extinct volcano which stands guarding the harbour of Honolulu, Hawaii. This poem was written by a boy who had just attended such a concert:

Crater Celebration

The blaring bands in my mind,
Peaceful, tranquil so I find:
To yell and scream without a care,
To get away from squeezing strings,
My sudden freedom really rings.
(W.L., Iolani School, Honolulu, Hawaii)

Anzac Day

Anzac Day is celebrated in Australia each April 25. It commemorates a First World War disaster at Gallipoli, and the sacrifice made by many Australian soldiers there. A young man in Sydney writes as follows:

Anzac Day

Wooden faced old men come from hibernation
Of quiet homes to wear their gaudy
Lives of tin and ribbon,
    and limp the streets
in age old triumph,
Absorbing one day a year of life.
(J.M., Sydney Grammar School, Sydney, Australia)

Horse Racing

Horse racing is a popular pastime in many countries. In this poem, an Australian boy gives his impressions of a day at the races:

Race Day

Dust hangs over the track,
And there's tension in the air—
The colorful clothes, the mighty horses,
The cool beer flowing:
The gun is fired,
The horses thunder—
And it's on again.

(A.T., Brisbane Grammar School,
Brisbane, Australia)

Chinese New Year

Chinese New Year is a colourful occasion celebrated every February. Here James Lee, a pupil at Iolani School in Honolulu, describes the occasion as it happens in Hawaii:

Streets are lined with people;
The gong sounds,
The drum rolls,
The lion dances up and down;
Fireworks crackle:
Festivities begin.

Young people everywhere seem to be interested in laughter, gaiety, and ceremony. Capitalize on this interest by getting them to write about some celebration of their choice.

Song of Thanks

How easy it is to be pessimistic about things, to be cynical and negative. At a time when many of the forces around us seem to be destructive, it is important that we as teachers try to dwell upon constructive influences and that we encourage our young people to do so as well.

Ask your pupils to write a short song of thanks. Caution them against insincere expression. They should say only those things that they mean.

Thanks for sadness
that makes happiness much brighter;
Thanks for the storm
that clears the next day;
For without some bad,
Good would be meaningless.

(B.W., Putney School, Putney, U.S.A.)

Thanks for love,
For buttered popcorn,
for all things that try
    to be warm and beautiful;
Thanks for letting me see,
    not merely look;
Thanks for letting me be myself;
Thanks.

(R.A., Monklands High School,
Montreal, Canada)

Thank you for rain,
sun,
flowers,
freedom—
There are so many good things:
If you look,
You'll find them.

(G.P., The Dragon School,
Oxford, England)

The American poet Langston Hughes captures much of the intended spirit of this section in his poem "Dreams":

Hold fast to dreams,
For if dreams die,
Life is a broken-winged bird,
That cannot fly.

Hold fast to dreams,
For when dreams go,
Life is a barren field,
Frozen with snow.

4. Making a Poem

After spending many pleasant hours developing their potential for expression and observation, beginners eventually ask the question: "Teacher, is what I have done any good?" The best way I have found to answer that question is to plot, from scratch, the making of a poem. By the end of the process the criteria of evaluation should become quite clear.

As opposed to the focus of the earlier descriptive sections, here at the evaluation stage our pupils must be conscious of the distinction between *what* they have said and *how* they have said it. What they have said is their content, the substance of their feelings, and hence is a part of themselves. How they have said it is their technique, the craft of their expression. It is in this second area that they should hope to make advances and improve.

Making a Poem Class Session

I shall start off the chapter by presenting you with another sample class session. (See also Chapter 2.) This one explores more fully than the first the evaluation dimension. Please keep in mind as before that every class period is a unique "happening"—a never-to-be-exactly-repeated combination of activities and interactions. Every teacher is an individual who is developing his/her own approach. Hence attempting to detail what might happen in a "typical period" is a risky undertaking. Nevertheless, let me try to outline the progress of a class focusing on the theme of Making a Poem.

Teacher: You know, boys and girls, making a poem is a little like baking a cake. Before you start your cake, you need some kind of a recipe. You must know how many cups of flour and sugar you need, how much butter, flavouring, and so on. Then you need to know how to mix these ingredients such as "stir in the milk, and beat rapidly for three minutes." Finally you need to know how long to bake the mixture such as "place in a hot oven and leave for 30 minutes."

John: That sounds easy, teacher.

Teacher: Don't be misled, John. Making anything, particularly a poem, is never easy; but it does involve certain skills that can be learned and developed with experience. Now what could we say is the first ingredient of our "poem recipe"?

Mary: First we have to decide what we're going to write about. We have to pick a subject.

Teacher: Good, Mary. In the same way we would decide whether we wanted to bake an orange cake, or a chocolate one, so we have to decide what the topic of our poem is going to be. Let's put something up on the blackboard here. What could we call this whole area?

Joan: How about content?

Teacher: I like it, Joan. Let's put up the heading *content* on this half of the board. Now we can consider what we are going to write about.

George: May we write about anything we want?

Teacher: Of course you may, George; anything that interests you or captures your attention. Be careful though not to pick a subject that is so large that you won't be able to achieve any focus in your writing.

Jane: What do you mean by *focus*, teacher?

John: I think he means getting detail such as a photographer tries to when he adjusts his lens. I take pictures myself, and I always have to measure distances and think about focus so I can capture precise details.

Teacher: That's exactly right, John. As writers we must try to set our subjects up like photographers do. Let me share an illustration with you. One morning several years ago I was in Sydney, Australia, at Cranbrook, a fine school on Bellevue Hill, overlooking the opera house, bridge, andharbour. I had been invited by the art master to come and see him working with his class of seven year olds. I arrived a little late, so when I got there the pupils had easels set up with big pieces of paper on them. Paint and brushes were at their side. As I came up the path to the garden where they were working, I noticed that each pupil had a piece of cardboard in his hand with a small square cut from the centre of it. They were all holding these pieces of cardboard at arm's length and looking through them. What do you think they were doing?

Mary: They were finding their subjects. With kids of that age if you take them to the top of a hill and show them a wide view—like the harbour you are telling us about—they'll probably try to put it all into their picture, and it will end up a mess.

John: That's right. They won't have any focus. The teacher probably said to them, "Look through your squares, and anything you see there you can put in your picture. If it isn't in your square it can't be in your picture."

Teacher: Mary and John, you're quite right. That's exactly what the teacher had said, and so the kids that day did some pictures on aspects of Sydney Harbour that had real focus. It is much too big a subject to get on one piece of paper in any detail.

George: Give us a subject that we might write about today, teacher.

Teacher: I don't want to do that, George. I'd like you to pick your own subject. But perhaps I could make a couple of suggestions before you start. For example don't try to write about a polar bear or a Thompson's gazelle. Why not?

George: I probably don't know enough about them. I have seen polar bears on TV, but I don't know what a Thompson's gazelle is!

Teacher: The Thompson's gazelle is like a small antelope, George. If you lived on the Serengheti Plains of East Africa you could probably write about him with no trouble at all. You'd know him—his colour, movements, actions, and personality. So remember, try to pick some subject that you really know and like. Then you'll be able to make it come alive on your page more easily. Otherwise writing may be difficult.

Joan: Could I write about a whole number of my subject, teacher? I live on a farm, and I'm thinking about fenceposts.

Teacher: That's a fine question, Joan. When you think about the subject fenceposts (plural) what do you see in your mind's eye? What picture do you get?

Joan: Just a whole collection of posts running away into the distance.

Teacher: Do you see any detail? Anything specific?

Joan: Not really. Just a lot of pieces of wood.

Teacher: Exactly, Joan. And that usually happens when we think about a subject that is plural. We lose the detail. But suppose I ask you to think about fencepost (singular). What do you see? Describe it for me.

Joan: Well, it's an old post with a kind of stringy wood falling off it, and some cobwebs in the chinks at the top.

Teacher: Very good, Joan. Does it have any colour?

Joan: Yes, it's grey, and darker brown near the bottom. It looks as though the termites have been at it.

Teacher: Is there anything else on it?

Joan: Yes. A rusty old bit of barbed wire about half-way up. One end of the wire is snapped off and is just sticking into the air. It looks lonely.

Teacher: And how about around the bottom? Is there carefully mowed grass?

Joan: Oh, no. It's all rough and matted. The grass is long and coarse and looks a bit like a jungle. There's even some fungus on the post. Nobody's done much about looking after it.

Teacher: Good, Joan. Do you see what's happened? You got some fine details when you thought about fencepost, but very little when you thought about a whole number of them. Maybe George, if we pick the singular of whatever our subject is going to be, we'll have better focus.

Tim: Are we going to put anything else on the board under *content*?

Teacher: Good question, Tim. What do you think we might include?

Tim: Well, what the subject looks like?

Teacher: Fine, you've suggested a whole area here, Tim, that is most important. You're talking about the senses. Let's see if we can name the five senses.

Tim:	Sight.
George:	Sound.
Mary:	Feel.
Fred:	Smell.
Ann:	Taste.
Teacher:	Very good. I've written them all up here on the board. Now let's see if we can add one or two things beside these senses; something to give us a little further help in writing about our subject. Tim, when you suggested *sight* what kinds of details were you thinking about?
Tim:	Colour, for one. We spoke about the grey and brown fencepost. Probably shape as well. Mary told us about pieces falling off the post and the termite holes.
Teacher:	Very good, Tim. I've put these up beside *sight* on our list. How about *feel* Mary? What could we add beside yours?
Mary:	I was thinking about things like movement and action. Does the subject move in a special way? I could write about its action: what it does.
Teacher:	These are all excellent suggestions. And you know they are really just guidelines, things to think about when you are considering your subject? If you can't include anything on taste or smell let's say, don't worry. You just want a kind of checklist of senses as you go along. Perhaps there's at least one more heading we should include on this side under *content*. Can you suggest anything?
Ann:	How about *character* or *personality*? I think we should be trying to give something of the texture of our subject —what it is like from the inside-out. I'm always interested in reading about things if they seem real to me, if they have a soul.
Teacher:	What a thoughtful contribution, Ann. Probably in any effective piece of writing we should get a feeling for its personality, texture, or soul, as you say. Let's put that up

122

on the board here and try to think about it as we are writing today.

Now, let's get back to the idea of the "poem recipe" that we started with. We've talked about the content of our recipe, what we might put into our poem, or what it is going to be about. Now what other main ingredient might we put on the right side of the board, here?

Edward: We really haven't said anything yet about the structure of our poem, what shape it's going to take. We've got to know something about that.

Teacher: Quite right, Edward. I like one of the words you used there very much—*structure*. Let's use it as the heading for our right side. The structure will tell us something about the form our poem might take.

Edward: Does a poem have to be very long, teacher?

Teacher: That's a good question, Edward. The quick answer is, certainly not. In fact, poems often differ from prose in that they are shorter, more concise. Where a sentence often stretches the whole way across our page, a poem is usually tighter, often containing only two or three words per line. Let's try to keep our lines tight, and the length of our poems to five lines at the most.

John: That will probably be a bigger challenge than writing a whole lot anyway. It's often more difficult to put something in a few words than to go on and on about it.

Teacher: How right you are, John. Do you remember the lovely story about Voltaire? Apparently he had written a very long letter to a friend of his, and closed it by saying "I am sorry that this letter is so long. If I had had more time, it would have been shorter." Perhaps making a poem is a little bit the same. What word could we put up on the board to remind us of what we have been talking about here?

Joan: Why not just put *shape*, and then in a bracket after it *concise, tight,* that will remind us.

Teacher: Thanks, Joan. I've already written your suggestion up here.

123

Brian: Does the poem have to rhyme?

Teacher: That's a useful question, Brian.

Darcy: Of course, it doesn't. Only nursery rhymes rhyme. I can say what I want better if I don't have to bother about rhyme. It's more natural to me without it.

Teacher: I'm glad you feel that way, Darcy. I would encourage you not to worry about rhyme unless you really want to have it. There is one ingredient in our "poem recipe" that is probably far more important than rhyme, however. Can anyone suggest what it is?

Sue: I'd say it would be rhythm. Lots of poems don't have rhyme, but most poems have some kind of rhythm. It's the way their words move.

Teacher: Excellent, Sue. Let's put that word *rhythm* up on the board. I particularly like that statement you just made— "It's the way their words move." That's just what rhythm is and it's something we must listen for in any poem.

(The blackboard now might look something like this):

Content

Subject You Know
Focus
Sight –   colour
          shape
Sound
Feel –   movement
         action
Smell
Taste
Character – texture, soul

Structure

Shape – concise
        tight

Rhythm

Detail

Teacher: Now I think we're almost ready to do some writing of our own, don't you? Just before you pick your subject, have a look at these pictures *(holding them up in front of the class).*

124

Here's one of a lion, the simba, taken with a telephoto lens in East Africa. What do you notice in particular about it?

Tim: I don't know whether he is roaring or yawning, his mouth is so wide-open; but the detail is amazing. It looks as if he has road maps on his tongue.

Teacher: Here's another picture of a frog jumping for a dragonfly. Notice how the frog appears to be frozen in his jump with the water suspended in air in the background.

John: That picture must have been taken at a shutter speed of less than a thousandth of a second. I know from my own camera. Look at the dragonfly's wings. They are completely stopped in the picture and they move.

Teacher: Here's a picture of the edelweiss, that magnificent highland flower, taken by Pierre Tainaz, the most famous of Alpine photographers. He took this picture near his home at Chamonix in the French Alps. What do you notice particularly about it?

Ann: It's the petals and tendrils; the detail of them is so intricate. The lighting effect makes them look like a spider web, a net spun of the finest threads.

Teacher: Apparently, Ann, Pierre Tainaz sat for four hours with his shutter at the ready, waiting for the sun to produce the exact combination of light and texture you are talking about. He calls it "capturing the moment."
As we've seen from these few pictures, inspiration can be found anywhere if our eyes are wide-open. Would some people like to bring in a few pictures so we could have a look at them another time?

All: Give us a few days to collect some.

(I would suggest that all teachers and class groups try to build collections of pictures. This activity should help to direct attention to everyday observations.)

Teacher: Now that we have concentrated on the detail in these pictures, let's try to pick a subject and develop our own detail in words. Perhaps I could make a few suggestions of topics that might trigger some ideas for you. If you hear one you like, pick it, and write a short poem on it. If you don't hear anything you like, select your own topic, of course.

crow	shirt pattern	seagull
dirt road	shadow	bush fire
spider web	snow drift	shanty
junk yard	orange peel	baby
lightning	shark	pebble
grain-in-wood	fog	oily puddle
tree stump	sand crab	fallen leaf

Julie: When you said "tree stump," it reminded me of the Douglas fir. We used to live in British Columbia. May I write about the Douglas fir?

Teacher: Of course, Julie, you know it well, a fine subject.

Mary: I'm going to do my poem on caribou. We went up to Baffin Island last holidays. How long should it be?

Teacher: Remember we decided to keep the pieces short and tight, Mary. Let's say five lines long at the most. Try to keep your lines concise, perhaps only two or three words per line. I'll give you a little time now to write. Please don't talk during this time. You'll need to concentrate if you are going to do something that pleases you. Each one of you has your own individual ideas, so talk will disturb the others. At the end of the writing period, I'd like to call on a number of you to read your pieces aloud. So remember as you are making your poem, try to hear it in your head; say it to yourself. When you have finished your first draft, rework it, trim it perhaps. This is certainly not an exercise in "instant poetry." You'll probably want more time after this period to polish your piece. But at least we can make a start now.

Tim: I understand what we're trying to do. Could you just read us one or two examples done by others to give us an idea of rhythm and the tightness we've been talking about?

Teacher: Thanks for asking, Tim. I was just about to read you
several pieces. Try to tune your ear to them and hear the
rhythm. After I've read them—and you'll notice I read
them slowly because poetry must be read slowly—start
on your own piece without any more questions. I'm sure
you're going to make something you like today. Now
listen carefully.

*(Remembering the criteria we are trying to establish with our
young writers—to be elaborated shortly—we teachers should
develop a growing collection of pieces made by our pupils for use
as examples at times such as these.)*

Bush

**Silent, stunted
Stubby, blackened branches;
Leaves grey and shrivelled;
Burnt-out bush.**

*The Dive of the Wedge-Tail**

*Streaks of colour
Plummeting earthwards—
Talons outstretched.*

Gooseberry

A thorny bush;
A sour green fruit;
An inquisitive hand;
Some jam on toast.

Parched Ground

**The earth,
Solid;
Places split jagged;
Lifeless tufts without grip.**

*This poem is discussed on pp. 130-131 and p. 152.

Teacher: Now go ahead and make your own piece.

(The time available for writing in most class periods will be short, probably only ten to fifteen minutes at most. This time limitation can act as a positive influence. The here-and-now urgency of the situation creates a "sense of occasion" which in fact helps the majority of young writers in their enterprise.)

Teacher: I'm sorry our time has been short today, and that we've all been a bit rushed. But I'm excited as I look around to see that most of you have got something on your papers. I'm proud of the way you have been concentrating. Many of you were able to lose yourselves in your subjects and so escape from the four walls of this classroom. That's really what counts you know. Don't be discouraged if you haven't produced a gem in these few minutes. It's most unlikely. Writing doesn't happen easily, does it? The important thing is that you've gotten involved, and developed some ideas to work toward. It may be weeks or months before you write a poem that pleases you; but when you do, that will be part of the result and reward of today's work.

George: May a few of us read the pieces we've done?

Teacher: Thanks for asking, George. I'm glad you want to, because that's really the best way to make your pieces come alive. A poem like a gramophone record needs to be heard to make it live.

Doris: That's true, isn't it? My favourite Elton John record is just a piece of plastic till I can put it on the turntable and let it play.

Teacher: Exactly, Doris. But remember, you are the only one at the moment who knows exactly how to breathe life into your poem. You know what you have tried to say, so read your piece slowly, and with the kind of expression that will help us to understand it. You must try to interpret your words for us. The difference between Paul Scofield and an eight-year-old schoolboy saying "Friends, Romans, countrymen, lend me your ears" is probably mainly in interpretation. Paul Scofield lives the words—he almost gets inside them—and that helps us

to understand their significance. Try to do the same
when you read from your poem. Who'd like to start?
Thanks, Ann. Give us your title first and then your piece.

Ann: Nullabor Plain

              Scars spurting open:
              Cracking from the sun;
              Jagged, rough-like;
              Coated in thick, red soil.

Teacher: Very good, Ann. I like your tight rhythm and the feeling
           of harshness you have created. Have you ever been out
           on the Nullabor?

Ann: Yes, I went across it in a caravan with my parents at the
           last holiday. It was fascinating.

John: Brown-booker Kangaroo

              Bounding, running scared,
              Blending against trees,
              Hiding,
              Eyes glittering fear.

Teacher: A very fine piece, John. You have really captured the
           spirit of the kangaroo in your writing. I particularly like
           your last line: "Eyes glittering fear." That "glittering" is a
           well-chosen word.

*(I would suggest that encouragement of their efforts is one of the
most effective ways of motivating our young writers. This is particularly important in the early stages when they are making a leap of
faith in trusting us with their thoughts and feelings. I try to comment on any positive aspect of a piece even if this might be only
two or three words in one of the lines. Very few poems have absolutely no praiseworthy features.)*

Tim: Outback River*

              Long, meandering stretch;
              White sand blotched with patches of brown;
              Droopy box-gums shade the water holes;
              A blessing to the sunburnt swaggy;
              He lies in the water,
              Soaking up its cool friendship.

*This poem is mentioned on p. 152.

Teacher: Tim, I like your piece very much, particularly the vivid picture you paint of the river in the first three lines. The colour in your second line is excellent, and the word "droopy" in the third line is most effective. Does anyone in the class have any comments to make about Tim's poem?

Michael: I like it very much, but I think it's a little too long. He lost me at the end. To me, the last two lines are an anti-climax. I'd like the poem to end after the fourth line.

Teacher: Thank you for your comments, Michael. Tim knows that you are not being critical of his piece—you said you liked it—but that you are trying to offer some constructive suggestions. What do you think of his idea, Tim?

Tim: Looking at it again, I think I agree with Michael. The last two lines are probably a bit off the subject anyway. I really said what I wanted to say in the fourth line.

Teacher: I'm glad you agree with Michael, Tim, because I think he's made a valuable point. It is usually a mistake to try to tell your readers everything. We mustn't insult their intelligence or restrict their opportunities for interpretation. If you end your poem with the line "A blessing to the sunburnt swaggy," then each reader can have his own interpretation of what that "blessing" is. You let your reader empathize with your poem yet you don't try to force his/her attitude too much.

Tim: I think the poem also has more punch if it ends after the fourth line. It has more impact there.

Teacher: Exactly. Let me share with you a similar example. You remember that poem I read a few minutes ago "The Dive of the Wedge Tail" (p. 127)? Well the first version of that poem actually went like this:

> Streaks of colour
> Plummeting earthwards—
> Talons outstretched:
> Shrieks of terror
> Terrible, violent death.*

*For further discussion of this poem see p. 152.

George: I like it better without the last two lines. When he ends with "talons outstretched," it lets us use our imagination; each person can put in his/her own gory ending!

Teacher: That's just the point, George. The boy who wrote this poem, after he had a chance to rework it, also felt it had more impact when it ended after the third line.

Ann: That's very interesting. He improved it when he reworked it didn't he? Would you say we should always rework our pieces?

Teacher: Yes, I'd say so. Ann. Even if you don't alter much or anything, it's always wise to go over your first version, and try to polish. Professional writers do. Let's look at another example while we are on this subject. Remember that poem I read you yesterday on "Ghost Gum"? Here is how it looked in its original form:

> Pale, ghostly gum
> Leaves rippling, rustling
> In the gentle breeze;
> Gnarled twisted branches
> Begging to the sky for rain.*

And here is how it looked in its final version:

> Pale ghostly gum,
> Leaves rustling:
> Gnarled twisted branches—
> Begging the sky for rain.

Mary: I'm glad David tightened it up. That third line particularly —"In the gentle breeze"—that's a real cliché. And that word "rippling" too. That wasn't doing anything for his originality.

Teacher: Good girl, Mary. You remember what we said last week about clichés. I was particularly pleased when the writer of this poem decided to eliminate the word "to" from the last line.

*For further discussion of this poem see pp. 151-152.

Michael: It may seem like a small change, but to me, it makes a tremendous difference to his rhythm. The line just doesn't seem to work when the "to" is there.

Teacher: Eureka, Michael! Now you're really starting to hear the music of the words. Could we listen to a few more poems in our closing minutes? Let's enjoy the pieces people have made today.

Greg:
Gum Nut*

Suspended beneath coarse grey twigs,
Searching for survival;
Dependent on the heaving boughs
Between so many boasting leaves.

All: Gasp. . . . Greg, that's a beauty. That word "boasting" is just right for the leaves.

(Greg has come last in his English group for the past several years. His classmates are amazed at what he has accomplished here. Happily, this sort of thing happens quite frequently. The achievement of self-esteem for Greg far transcends the value of simply making a poem. It brings him a new dignity which will probably lift him in everything he attempts to do.)

Benjamin:
Morning Glory

The morning glory
Which blooms for an hour
Differs not at heart
From a tree
Which lives for a hundred years.

Teacher: Benjamin, that's a wonderful thought, you have really captured the soul of an idea there. Thank you.

David:
The Foal: Newborn

Its moist matted coat
Cocoons its frail bones;
It struggles,
Wobbles—
A miracle.

*This poem is again cited on p. 149.

Teacher: David, that's beautiful. . . . Have you actually seen a foal being born? You must have from the way your poem lives.

David: Oh yes, many times. I live on a big property near Long-reach (Queensland), and my dad often asks me to help him about the place. It's terrific being close to nature.

Teacher: Boys and girls, we've had a good time together today. I think we've all learned a lot about writing: but more important, we've grown a lot, and learned more about ourselves and about one another. We'll all be able to walk out of this room a little taller than when we came in and a little richer inside. And that's wonderful. Thanks for sharing today. See you next time.*

*All the pieces quoted in "Making Poetry" were written by pupils from two Australian schools: one group at Downlands College, Toowoomba, Queensland; and the other at Marist School in Bunbury, Western Australia. In neither group did the young writers have more than ten minutes in which to complete their work.

Know Your Subject

Be Interested in Your Subject

The selection of a topic poses two potential problems for any beginner. First, the young writer may have been preconditioned to believe that poetry is something special, that the material of the poet's interest lies exclusively in the realness of "daffodils," "clouds," and "immortality."

Young writers must understand that any topic is an acceptable basis for a poem, whether this be ice hockey, space travel, pop music, clothes lines, or caribou. The major concern should be their own personal interest in the subject. If a boy in Montreal admires Guy Lafleur as an ice hockey player and wants to write about his flashing blades and slashing shots, encourage him to do so. It's his choice; no area of interest should be outlawed. Perhaps the boy who wishes to write about Lafleur has a field of interest centring on hockey players at this time. Let him start where his present enthusiasm lies. Probably at some future date his horizons will broaden—so much the better—but don't try to force the process!

Know Your Subject First Hand

Secondly, young people must remember that they can probably write with impact only about those topics that they really know. It would be difficult for a Canadian girl to try to write about a cheetah. Unless she has spent some time in East Africa, or a long time in zoos, she probably doesn't know enough about the cheetah to provide the necessary details. Her piece won't come alive. Conversely, it would be difficult for African youngsters to write about elk.

Encourage your pupils then to pick topics that they themselves have an interest in—whatever the area of that interest may be—but stress that they should know a good deal about the subjects that they choose, preferably through experience at first hand.

Recently I had an unusual experience which helps to illustrate this point. I was conducting an evening writing session at an inner city boarding school in New York City. There were 20 fourteen-year-old boys in the group, with a large delegation of teachers as observers. We had talked about the world of nature and the many natural beauties of America. I had encouraged the boys to pick a topic from one of six general areas—animals, birds, insects, fish, plants, and trees. They were to choose something that they knew well enough to be able to provide details about; I asked them not to consult one another in any way and gave them ten minutes in which to compose their poems.

At the end of the ten minutes, proceedings went something like this:

"Thanks for working so well tonight, boys, and for concentrating on your writing. Now I suggested six major areas from which you might pick your topic. Just for interest—because I know you haven't consulted one another about this—let's have a show of hands as to what areas you've picked. Who has written about an animal?"

(Not a single hand goes up.)

"Who has written about a bird?"

(Not a hand.)

"Who has written about an insect?"

(Nobody.)

"Who has written about a fish?"

(Nineteen hands out of twenty go up.)

"This is amazing! I know you didn't talk to one another about this. Can anybody explain to me why almost all of you have written about fish? I would have expected a pretty even division on all six of the areas."

"Mr. Powell, you suggested that we write about something that we know. This is a boarding school in downtown New York City. We are able to leave here only one day a month, Sunday, and on that day Father Tyler usually takes us down to the shore to do some fishing. It's great, and we get catfish and perch and flatheads. I decided to write about fish because I know them best. If you look around there aren't many animals or birds what with all these smokestacks and concrete. I don't really know any of those other things you mentioned."

"Thanks, Tim. That explains it. You were quite right not to pick a subject you didn't know".

Obviously the boys made the most appropriate choices. Though they may have been to the Bronx Zoo, they really didn't *know* any of the animals there. Apart from its interest as an example in subject selection, I find this situation a fascinating and somewhat tragic commentary on urban life in the seventies.

Be Enthusiastic

When young people are writing about subjects they know and like, their work exudes an enthusiasm, a *joie de vivre.* Take the following two poems for example. Steve, who wrote this first one, is a canoe enthusiast. He attends Phillips Exeter Academy in Exeter, New Hampshire, and uses every weekend he can get to explore the water and wilderness north of his school. Building his own canoes, he appreciates the subtleties of their design.

Canoe

Ribs of wood
Joined to a backbone—
Spindly skeleton;
Tight canvas skin
Burnt brown in the sun
Streamlined:
Let's go.

Tim is an Australian boy who like many of his mates, loves the water. He goes swimming and surfing at Manly Beach on the north shore of Sydney Harbour, but most of all he enjoys the excitement of competitive sailing.

Ocean Racing
Ploughing, surging down the trough;
Pushing, ramming into the crest;
Billowing sails, they pull to their mast;
Pushlng, ramming into the crest.

If the two poems just quoted transmit any enthusiasm—and I believe they do—a large part of their success lies in the fact that their writers know and have been part of their subjects.

Experience It

It is probably of little use to ask a boy who has never been out in white water to write about the thrills of kayaking. Therefore I would strongly advocate that whenever possible, you bring your pupils into direct contact with what they are going to write about. Take them for an afternoon walk in the autumn woods. Take them to a busy city intersection. Take them for a run in the park or up some hills. Then they'll have something to write about at first hand.

Encourage your pupils to be constantly attentive to the things around them. There are poems everywhere.

Focus

Be they photographers, painters, or writers, all creative artists must be conscious of focus. Similar to the plight of a photographer who takes pictures without having his/her lens properly set, young writers will miss the mark unless they have some focus and point of interest for their poetry. Let's consider several ways of helping our pupils achieve focus in their writing:

Sequence of Words

The exact order of words is important to the precision of a statement and to the clarity of its meaning. Examine this poem written by a pupil at Putney School and already quoted in the "Contrast" section of this book (p. 93).

Wood/Plastic
Wood, soft,
Rubbed down to a rich-red brown
by a thousand hands.

After considering this original version, the young writer decided that his meaning would be clearer—his focus, sharper—if he altered the position of the phrase "to a rich-red brown." Consequently he rewrote his piece to read:

> Wood, soft,
> Rubbed down by a thousand hands
> To a rich red-brown.

This sequence of words improves not only the direction of his poem, but its rhythm as well.

Sequence of Items

Equally significant to the focus as the order of words is the sequence in which items are presented by the writer. These items are the ingredients of his poem—thoughts, ideas, details—and must be presented in an order which leads the reader to the heart of the writer's statement. The time sequence is significant. Several considerations are important in this regard.

A Strong Opening
Wherever possible, the writer should begin his piece with impact. He should start fast.

Geese

The geese in the sun
Grow larger in V's:
A hissing of wings—
And they're gone.
(Andrew Bicker, Canford School, Dorset, England)

In this poem, Andrew has opened with a strong visual image. We can immediately see his geese in our mind's eye.

A Well-Sustained Body
Any poem should present a type of progression—whether in action or thought—from start to finish. The beginning must be sustained and developed through the body of the poem if the piece is to have substance. The poem "Happiness" by the Hawaiian girl (p.83) is a good example here; so is this piece by a Canadian pupil:

Country Dawn

Country dawn—
Light blue reflections,
Golden-thread fingers spear the sky;
Eruption of sunlight,
Colours fly.
(J.M., Dunton High School, Montreal, Canada)

The writer here holds his poem together through an effective combination of observations based on a sequence in time.

A Conclusion With Impact

In some respects, the closing statement of any piece should carry its greatest impact. Readers tend to remember best what they hear last. Encourage your pupils to develop a strong conclusion, one that will stick.

Here are some examples of three different endings, each one distinctive its own way:

Metropolitan Boulevard

The steel gray snake
Winds its way
Past factories
Whose roof-top advertisements
Clutter the sky
With infinite words.

**(I.K., Monklands High School,
Montreal, Canada)**

Mini Skirt

What skirt?
Is that a skirt?
Are your sure it's a skirt?
WOW.

(T.P., Raffles Institution, Singapore)

Hair*

I want, like Jesus,
On my shoulders, down my back,
In its beauty, hair.

(P.J., The King's School,
Parramatta, Australia)

Focus is important to any artist, but particularly to the writer. Teach your pupils to approach their topics from some specific point of view, and to use this point of view to give direction to their expression.

---

*You will recognize in this poem the classical 5/7/5 syllable form of the Japanese haiku. For a description of how to handle the haiku in the classroom see *English Through Poetry Writing*.

Keep It Simple

In an age of magniloquence, simplicity of expression is a virtue. Our young writers should be helped to realize that the simplest way is usually the most effective way. Wasn't it Sir Winston Churchill who used to say to his advisers that if they couldn't make their reports to him on one side of paper, then they should go back and start again?

Study the following first draft of a poem by Geoffrey Baker of Blackwood High School in Adelaide, South Australia:

Preying Mantis

A motionless stick—waiting
Poised for the kill
Watching every move;
Waiting for the cracking of jaws:
The end has come.

A class discussion about this effort should uncover a number of obvious weaknesses in it. The basic idea is strong, but it is loosely expressed. The lines are somewhat disjointed in sequence, and the present order blunts the poem's impact. Although it is short the piece appears cluttered. Geoffrey worked at simplifying his expression, and eventually came up with the following version:

A motionless stick—waiting,
Watching every move,
Poised for the kill.

This final version is tighter, has a simpler time sequence, and hence strikes the reader with greater impact.

Katie Gibson of Casterton School in Kirkby Lonsdale, England, started with a good idea but a jumbled form of expression.

Storm

A storm appears
To be brewing in the sky;
There are streaks of lightning
And thunder is rumbling all around;
Soon it will be raining.

After considerable reworking and tightening, Katie produced the following simplified and more effective final version:

> *Thunder beating*
> *Lightning flashing*
> *The storm has broken—*
> *Rain.*

Read these two versions to your pupils. Even inexperienced writers will hear the difference between them, and the contrast should help them to simplify their own expression.

The Eskimos in the north of Canada have developed a poetry that is striking in its simplicity. Perhaps the harshness of their environment encourages them to be monosyllabic. Your pupils should benefit from listening to these pieces by Inuit poets:

> *Tundra Caribou*
>
> *A warmth of summer*
> *Sweeping over the land;*
> *Not a cloud;*
> *And among the mountains*
> *The grazing caribou.*

Winter

Hard times, dearth times,
Plague us every one;
Stomachs are shrunken;
Dishes are empty.

Making Songs

A wonderful occupation
Making songs:
But all too often
They are failures.

Most young people have a natural sense of rhythm. Much as they have an appreciation for the beat of music so they have a feeling for the flow of words. Hence the examples we read to them just before they are about to write should have a strong influence in helping them to make their own poems. If we stress simplicity and tightness of expression and read them poems that are good examples of these virtues, then it is more likely that our pupils will achieve simplicity in their own writing.

Hear Your Rhythm

Throughout this book we have been placing emphasis on rhythm. It is one of the distinguishing marks of poetry. Young people have it in them, and by careful direction, we can help bring it out in their writing.

Rhyme

While rhyme is an element of rhythm, I discourage young writers from attempting it unless they are insistent. Frequently their choice is based on the incorrect preconception that "all poems must rhyme." I believe that rhyme is an obstacle to inexperienced writers, and can produce false effects. Listen to this poem, introduced earlier on p. 76, by Peter Jones, a young man who is a talented artist and musician in addition to being a writer. In his first six lines he tries to achieve rhyme, and the result is some rather stilted, trite expression. As he gets into his piece, however, he abandons the rhyme, his natural sense of rhythm takes over, and he achieves a much more lively flow of words. Read this poem aloud:

Sunset

In the sunset
you might see
Little old women
Drinking tea.

Maybe you see
A beautiful tree,
As in the autumn
With colourful leaves.

But what I see
Is a tropical island;
The colours are like parrots' feathers,
And crabs are crawling in the sun.

But before my eyes it changes;
And then I see a bullfight
With the cape flashing in the sun;
At the other end I see dirt flying,
And then the scene dies.

(Peter Jones, Park School, Brandon, Canada)

The Beat of Your Lines

Each year in early March I take a return teaching trip to Phillips
Exeter Academy in New Hampshire, an outstanding independent
school where I once served on the faculty. During my ten days in
New England I always get to the Boston area and enjoy an
extended lunch with David McCord, one of America's best-known,
contemporary poets. To McCord, rhythm is one of the most
essential elements of living. It pervades everything he does.
Although in his mid-seventies, he still maintains his great
enthusiasm for bowling, a sport that demands rhythm in every
movement. Listen to what he says about it: "Poetry essentially is
rhythm. Most physical games are highly rhythmic; you couldn't
drive a car without it!"

In the reading of his poetry to children, he achieves a marvellous
flow in his words, which his listeners can—and do—emulate. He
claims that his own affinity for rhythm was developed by his
grandmother who read aloud to him the entire King James Version
of the Bible when he was a child. The music of its language rings in
him still.

This aspect of reading is most important. Let your young writers
hear poetry—both their own and that of others—being read
aloud. Encourage them to read slowly and to breathe life into their
words so as to make the meanings come alive. They should get
inside their poem and let its rhythmic heart beat.

Make sure that before every writing session you let your pupils
hear several poems that have distinctive rhythm. For instance you
might read a poem like the next one, "Crow," and then ask the
students to notice the effective mid-line pause after "We sat." They
should also notice the impact of the last line—a short one
consisting of words of one syllable—which seems to echo the
hurried wingbeats of the departing bird.

Crow

In the silence of the gold and green
We sat, watching the circling of
the crow:
We listened to his screaming
Till at last he seemed to tire
And flew home.

**(Janet Watson, Riverdale High School,
Montreal, Canada)**

The following poem, "Seagull," has strong alliteration in the first lines, appropriate to the soaring antics of its subject. Its final line also moves in a swooping, staccato fashion, a rhythm quite in keeping with the abandon of a fishing dive!

Seagull

Sleek and soft
Gliding high—
Then diving to survive
(Joanne Buckley, Casterton School,
Cumbria, England)

Ian Derrick, a fine young man who lives in Fiji, has achieved an almost faultless sound balance in his poem "Parrot." Read it aloud, slowly.

Parrot

The parrot repeats;
He hears and speaks;
A student at work;
Patterned speech.

The strength of his work lies partly in his syllable count. Your pupils should recognize that if his first line for example read: "The parrot repeats himself," then it would have too many beats to allow it to move in harmony with the other three lines. Likewise, if his final line were trimmed to the single word "speech," then its rhythm would be too abrupt. Ian's piece is distinguished because of the synchronized balance of its beat. Encourage your pupils to listen for and analyze the rhythm in everything they write.

Rewriting

One of the most important stages in the creation of any poem is the reworking and polishing of original expression. Experienced professional writers usually rework their material many times before they achieve satisfaction. This fact should underline the point for all beginners and encourage them always to review their original expression and to have the patience to persevere.

Let us examine, in no particular order of importance, some of the main points our young writers should be looking for as they polish their work.

Picking the Exact Word

Much of the impact of effective expression lies in hitting the verbal nail directly on the head. Let me use an example from my own experience to illustrate the alternatives that often exist in selecting the word.

In composing a sentence for the first page of this book, I needed to decide on a verb. Here is the framework of the sentence:

"As I was running through a grain field two hours later—and the falling sun seemed to be setting it aflame—the title. . . . "

After considerable thought I proposed the following five alternatives:

> came
> hit
> happened
> grew
> struck

As I have explained on the first page, I had just conducted a writing session with a fine group of students at a conference in Saskatoon. Two hours later I was running through a grain field when the title for this book flashed into my head. Which of the five verbs should I use to describe the "Eureka process" of that moment? Let me review my decision:

Came   This verb is rather too pedestrian for the context. It lacks the spark of originality I am seeking and is too slow in tone for the flash inspiration I am trying to describe.

Hit	Smacks of journalese, the jargon of the sportswriter. It is good as far as impact is concerned, but somewhat trite and perhaps even overdone for this context.
Happened	Too slow in connotation for what I am trying to say; not enough of the speed, the mental electricity of the occasion. The word is accurate but its tone doesn't convey the desired punch.
Grew	Same logic as applies for the verb "happened," only more so. This choice is slightly more original perhaps, but still too slow. The incubation process for the title has been going on in my head for months. The verb I want must describe the illumination stage.
Struck	This appears to be the best alternative for the context. It imparts the necessary speed and sense of urgency, while at the same time retaining a certain originality. Its tone and pace are right.

The process of selecting one verb for this context probably took upwards of several hours. Young writers must realize that the task of picking the right word is often painstaking, and demands patience and experience. I have detailed this single instance as an illustration of the process.

The craft of picking the exact word includes many dimensions of course. The example just cited deals primarily with what we might call tone. We must also be concerned with the accuracy of the words we pick. Are they true to fact? A young man recently wrote the following piece:

Thistle

Prickly, long, deadly,
Silently swaying,
Growing, choking,
Deadly enemy.

May one honestly describe a thistle as "deadly"? Admittedly the prickles of the thistle are uncomfortable, unpleasant, but surely not "deadly." After reconsidering his choice, the young writer admitted that his word probably stretched his credibility with his readers. It was an unwise exaggeration created in the heat of excitement.

Often the inspired choice of a single word—one that has a particularly original or imaginative flair—can lift the quality of a whole piece. Such is the case with the poem by Greg of Bunbury, Western Australia, discussed in the "Making Poetry" selection (p. 132):

Gum Nut

Suspended beneath coarse grey twigs,
Searching for survival;
Dependent on the heaving boughs
Between so many boasting leaves.

Greg's choice of the word "boasting" is particulary appropriate for his context. Through it, he achieves a freshness of approach and an originality to be emulated.

Achieving Specific Detail

Young writers on reworking their pieces should always ask the question "Does my poem contain sufficient specific detail to make it come alive?" They should check for colour, movement, action, and the like, making sure that if their piece does not at the moment contain these details, then they should add them.

Recently a young boy produced the following piece:

Junk Yard

The din,
The mess,
The amount of waste
In such a space:
Amazing, fantastic
Not wanted any more.

(Peter Howe, Sandroyd School,
Wiltshire, England)

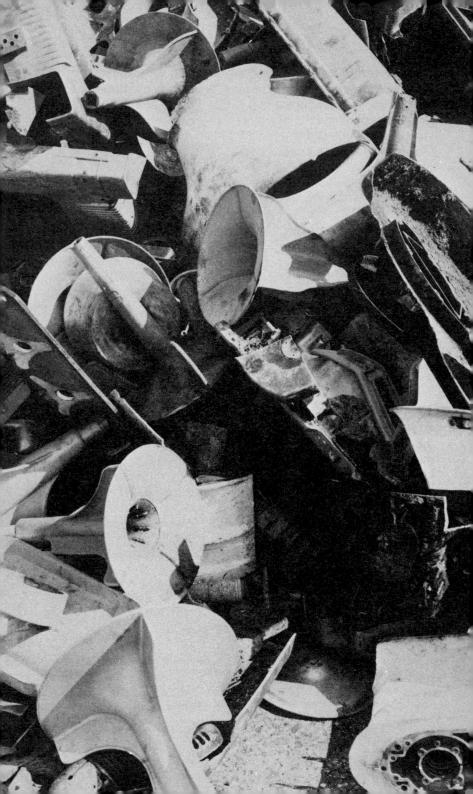

After some discussion, Peter agreed that he had not included any specific details such as crushed tin cans, distorted automobile frames, rusty coat hangers, or whatever. While the rhythm of his piece is reasonable, it does not really come alive because of its lack of specifics.

Peter then decided to start again, and rewrote his piece as follows:

Junk Yard

Rusty automobiles,
Crashed up wagons,
Crooked nails,
Scruffy old springs —
Rats.

Avoiding the Trite

Effective expression usually has a sparkle of originality, the flair of the unusual. Inexperienced writers should be encouraged to steer clear of shopworn, tired phrases. The cliché must be hunted down like a weed in a garden and as far as possible, cut out. A few carefully chosen examples should serve to underline this point: "The sun, a flaming orange ball, sinks slowly in the west."

David Kruger's poem "Ghost Gum," discussed previously on pp. 131-132, provides a strong example here:

Pale ghostly gum,
Leaves rippling, rustling
In the gentle breeze;
Gnarled twisted branches
Begging to the sky for rain.

151

His third line is most unfortunate. David decided to eliminate it. He also decided that the word "rippling" in his second line lacked freshness. His rewritten version is far stronger:

Pale ghostly gum,
Leaves rustling:
Gnarled twisted branches—
Begging the sky for rain.

Creating Impact Through Not Telling All

Young writers often need to be convinced of the value of restraint. They frequently lose impact by trying to tell their readers everything, and by leaving little to the imagination. Take the original version of the poem by Peter of Bunbury, Western Australia, as an example:

The Dive of the Wedge Tail*

Streaks of colour
Plummeting earthwards—
Talons outstretched:
Shrieks of terror
Terrible, violent death.

Peter's last two lines restrict our freedom of interpretation. He is insulting our intelligence by continuing after "talons outstretched." If he stops there, his piece has impact. We can all imagine the ending and fill in the details for ourselves.† Things unsaid are often more powerful than things said.

---

* This poem has been mentioned on p.127 and pp.130-131.
† The same principle holds true for the poem "Outback River" quoted and discussed earlier on pp.129-130.

Trimming: Achieving Tightness of Rhythm

Young writers should be encouraged to trim their original expression, to cut down on the number of their words in order to achieve tightness of rhythm. Suggest that they say their poems to themselves as they write so as to hear their rhythm. Listen more closely to David's poem:

Pale ghostly gum,
Leaves rippling, rustling
In the gentle breeze;
Gnarled twisted branches
Begging to the sky for rain.

When he said the last line over to himself, David realized that it was cluttered, that it contained too many syllables. By eliminating a single word, he achieved the flow he wanted: "Begging the sky for rain"

Tim did a comprehensive trimming of his poem "Morning":

The crowing of the bright red rooster
Breaks open the lonesome peace
Of the early country morning.

When he reviewed his piece, Tim felt that it was somewhat loose in rhythm and perhaps insulting to his readers in that it attempted to fill in too many of the details. He rewrote his piece as follows:

A rooster calls
Breaking the peace
Of morning.

Encourage your young writers to rework their original pieces a number of times, each time with a specific purpose in mind.

Rewriting After Hearing Other Poems on the Same Topic

Although the act of creation is an individual process, pupils benefit from hearing what their classmates have written on the same topic. Suggest a subject to your class — a dirt road, junk yard, bulldozer, or maple tree, for instance — and ask everyone to write a short piece about it. Then let each member of the class read his/her poem aloud. Encourage all the students to listen carefully and then, without any class discussion, to rewrite their own pieces. They should understand that they are not obliged to make any changes if they are satisfied with their original versions. Perhaps in hearing a number of other poems on the same subject, their perspectives will have been altered or reinforced or expanded in some way. After all, many minds are usually better than one.

As an example of this idea, read the work of two girls from different English classes at Phillips Exeter Academy. Each girl wrote a first version, listened to the poems of her classmates on the same topic, and then rewrote her own, including a prose comment at the end about what she had tried to do.

(i)

Stone wall
Orders feet;
Rocks tumble off, pushed —
Hard and jagged edges.

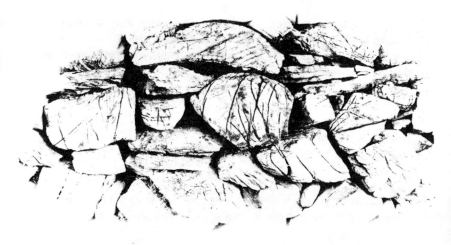

(ii)

Stone wall—
Unordered pattern orders feet;
Sides tumble, pushed;
Harsh and scraping edges.

"Stone walls are so varied. I found I had to put blinkers on and do one specific wall, and not stone walls in general. I think my second poem is more effective because I can feel in it more of the rambling quality of the wall. I didn't change the idea too much after the readings, but tried to rewrite mine with minor changes, rather than add several different ideas from others. I could see and enjoy most of the stone walls of the others, but I think I selfishly liked mine better, and just rebuilt it."

Anne Wheeler

(i)

Crow

With shiny blue-black coat
Screeching, perching, beseeching,
Coarsely crying bird,
Crow.

(ii)

Crow

Screeching,
Perched among the bare scraping branches
In a shiny, blackish-blue coat,
Coarsely crying bird.

"I like my second version better in that it has more continuity, and flows more easily than the first. It is more one continuous thought rather than disjointed segments of ideas. From my listening to the others, I got a clearer idea of simplicity of form. My problem was not having to cut down my first version—I used a bare minimum of words in it—but rather to elaborate on my ideas."

Julie Scolnik

Rewriting After Teacher-Directed Class Discussion

The follow-up to any writing session is almost as important as the creative period itself. You should encourage your pupils to look at their original pieces with a constructively critical eye. Experienced teachers often mimeograph copies of a number of poems and distribute these to every member of a class. The sheets can then be used as the basis of an analytic discussion.

As an example of the type of writing and comments that can arise, here are a number of poems on the topic of a junk yard. They were written at Phillips Exeter Academy and reproduced for a follow-up discussion by Mike Drummey, one of the outstanding young English instructors at the Academy:

(i)

Junk yard,
Filled with old unwanted's
All aging from the weather;
Always with new friends,
To be forgotten all together.

(ii)

Rotten fish,
Rotten foliage,
Fuming in the sunlight.

(iii)

Stinking, colorful,
Mixed-up pile,
Scavengers looking for prey.

(iv)

Tangled, twisted, rusting shards
    of broken metal,
Pile on pile of broken refuse,
Deathly still under a hot sun.

(v)

Piled with some of everything;
Always looks so crammed;
Everyone adding to it;
Few taking from it.

(vi)

Tin and rubber wastes
Piled up,
Spreading out,
Closed on Sunday.

(vii)

Objects of all sizes and shapes
Litter the hillside;
Rejects of civilization,
Rest to die.

The class discussion that followed produced a number of useful comments, and helped the pupils to formulate thoughts for their rewriting. The following abbreviated commentaries give some idea of the points that were raised:

(i) "Old unwanted's"—Rather clumsy; "new friends"—somewhat trite.

(ii) "Fish" and "foliage"—Are they really found in a junk yard, or aren't they more the contents of a compost heap? Has this writer stretched the topic too far?

(iii) Some strong imagery here.

(iv) The first image is particularly effective.

(v) Lack of specific detail is a weakness here; not one concrete item named.

(vi) Interesting approach. Is the final detail true to fact?

(vii) Last two lines perhaps overly vague, rather trite.

You as the teacher should determine the boundaries of such a discussion and direct it to fit the needs and abilities of your own class. Encourage your pupils to look at anything they write with an analytic eye, and always to be ready to rewrite where they see a more effective way. Part of the excitement of making poetry is the struggle to get the words right.

Is It Original?

One of the basic criteria for evaluating any piece of creative work is its originality. Does the piece ring with a new sound? Has it been struck in a new mint?

Convergent Versus Divergent Thinking

How does one encourage imaginative thinking in an age which places increasing emphasis on problem-solving, and the scientific method? To use the language of the educational psychologist, our pupils are becoming trained in convergent thinking, the process whereby they put on mental blinkers and zero in on a problem to the exclusion of any peripheral thoughts. Such thinking does not develop the imagination which depends for its nourishment on divergent thinking, the process of throwing open mental windows and letting the mind take any number of original courses.

If we are to encourage originality in our young writers, we must promote divergent thinking. We must stimulate our pupils to produce unusual answers to standard questions. In order to achieve this end, I have been working recently on a series of questions which I have been posing to children in sessions. They go something like this:

Teacher: Boys and girls, let's talk today about imagination. What is imagination?

Joan: It's when you make something up in your head.

John: It's fantasy—thinking about your dreams.

Tim: It's when you think of something that doesn't necessarily need to be true.

Teacher: These are all fine answers. Now let me ask you a few questions that are designed to challenge your imagination. Some of these questions may appear a little strange at first but remember there are no "right answers" to them. I want you to open your minds and let your imagination fly. Try to think up an answer that perhaps nobody else ever thought of before. Here's the first question: What could a giraffe use his neck for?

Mary: If a giraffe owned a kite, and if he went out flying it on a windy day and it got stuck up in the top of a high tree, then he could use his long neck to get his kite down with.

Teacher: Great idea, Mary. I like it.

George: If a giraffe goes out walking on the tarmac at the airport and if he sees a Jumbo jet standing over there with all those windows way up high, he can use his neck to look in the windows and see what's going on inside.

Teacher: Good boy, George. I'm glad nobody gave me the answer "to eat with" because that's a fact, isn't it? That wouldn't be imagination. Here are some other questions. Think about these.

Further Imaginative Questions

Where did the lion find his roar?

Why do butterflies fly crooked?

What kind of song does the lobster sing?

(This question was prompted by an answer given to me by a crippled youngster in a Montreal school. I had played to his class a band of tape containing the sound of waves crashing against a rocky shore, and I had asked the kids to say what they thought the sound was. John from his wheel chair put up his hand and said: "That's the song the lobster sings." I am sure you will find that questions *grow* for you in your classes much as this one did for me.)

What is the happiest animal anywhere, and why?

What does the colour yellow mean to you?

Give me an example of a zoomer, a splutterer, a purrer.

Where do shadows go at night?

What's it like at the bottom of
the sea?

Why does the grass grow green as
opposed to red, or purple, or white?

What are mud pies good for?

What's on the other side of the hill?

The reaction of young people to these questions is always a partial reflection of the kind of teaching to which they have been exposed. If most of the kids are scratching their heads and appear to be stopped in their tracks—"What do you mean by that question, teacher?"—this is probably an indication that they have been taught in a rather rigid, traditional method. If, however, as is usually the case, they find the questions are no problem, but rather an invitation to mental adventure, the indication is that they have been imaginatively taught and that divergent thinking is very much a part of their repertoire of skills. It is interesting to note that in most of the large-group sessions that I conduct containing both children and teacher-observers, it is usually the adults who find the questions puzzling, not the children. Most of today's young people seem to have an admirable mental flexibility which speaks highly for the improving standard of teaching they are receiving.

Open Your Mind

Make up your own questions with your own groups. The aim of the exercise is to encourage our young writers to think in an open way so that their minds are always ready to receive new ideas. It's a little like the fly-paper we used to hang up in country houses to catch summer flies. The paper used to come wrapped up in a tight cardboard cylinder and, in this state, would never catch anything. It had to be stretched out of the cylinder and left to hang, sticky and inviting, before it could do its job. The minds of young people must be open like the fly-paper before they can capture the many ideas that are in flight around them.

The Cliché

We started this section by talking about originality. Divergent thinking stimulates the imagination, and leads to originality of thought and expression. Encourage your pupils to search for the original phrase in their writing, to express their idea in a new way. Words that have been used too often are like guardsmen who have been called on to parade too many times. They are tired. They lack fire.

Discuss examples of clichés with your pupils. Get them to bring in examples of trite expression. If they are on the alert for them, eliminating time-worn phrases is not that difficult a task.

Originality extends to approach as surely as it does to the choice of words. See if your pupils can explain this piece:

Footprints

Footprints like mushrooms
On hard snow
Above the ground.
(Junsu Mitsima, Gordon Robertson
Educational Center, Frobisher Bay, Canada)

Junsu lives at Frobisher Bay on Baffin Island in the wind-swept Canadian Arctic. Each day he walks to school across the barren tundra. After a new snowfall, Junsu's mukluks leave footprints in the white surface, small craters where the snow has been compacted. As the wind howls, the lighter snow is gradually blown away from around these craters, eventually leaving them standing above the ground like mushrooms. Yesterday's footprints are now growing above the tundra. This observation by Junsu is a perceptive one. It provides a genuinely original basis for his poem.

Encourage your pupils to seek originality in their choice of subject and word. Freshness of approach should always be a major criteria by which to evaluate any piece of writing.

Is It Any Good?

Throughout this chapter we have tried in various ways to answer the question, Is my poem any good? By setting out some of the important factors that go into making poems, I have tried to provide standards of judgment for any piece of writing.

Content and Technique

At this point let me re-emphasize several concepts. First, we must always keep in mind the distinction between *what* I have written and *how* I have written it. The content of the piece usually contains the feelings or beliefs of the writer and as such is worthy of dignity. We may disagree with the opinion of a young writer, but as this opinion is part of him/herself, it is therefore out of bounds as far as literary criticism is concerned. English teachers have no place in evaluating the feelings of their pupils nor would they want to be called into this arena of judgment in my opinion.

The second dimension, the technique of the young writer, is a different matter, however. Writing is a craft, and as such demands certain skills which can be learned. Teachers of English are professionals in the development of these skills, and it is part of our responsibility to pass on these skills to our students.

Evaluation Review Questions

As a review of this chapter, let me propose a number of questions that all young writers might ask themselves in making or going over their poems. These questions should serve as a checklist and provide some measure for answering the question, Is my poem any good?

Do I know my subject well enough to write about it?

Am I really interested in it?

Have I got my subject in focus?

Have I presented specific details about it?

Is my expression simple and uncluttered?

Is my writing sufficiently tight?

Does my poem contain rhythm?

Have I read it aloud to hear my rhythm?

Should I eliminate any unnecessary words?

Do the words I have chosen convey my meaning as effectively as possible?

Is my piece original, imaginative?

Have I avoided clichés and tired phrases?

Have I reworked and polished my original several times over?

Do I like my final product?

Do It

In the final analysis, probably the most important objective for beginners or for advanced professionals for that matter is that they write and keep on practising their writing. It is largely through doing anything that we get better at it, whether this be playing the piano, kicking a football, reading a book, or writing poetry. So let's get on with the adventure.

5. Hallmarks of Creative Schools

The Qualities

My experience convinces me that there are several core qualities which, if they exist in a school, help it to become the kind of place where creative work flourishes. What are these core qualities?

A Caring Place

First, the school must be a caring place. Each pupil should have the feeling that he is somebody, that people respect his opinion. As a boy recently said to me about his school: "Everybody is somebody here." When each individual feels that he is being treated with dignity, that his opinion counts, then he is encouraged to give his best and to think about others at the same time.

An Atmosphere of Openness

Secondly, the school should have an atmosphere of tolerance and openness about it. Pupils should be free to express their opinions without fear of being condemned for their ideas or feelings. If young people are afraid to write what they really feel because of the negative reaction of classmates, then the atmosphere is not suitable for honest expression. A girl put her finger on this characteristic when she said: "We listen to each other here. No matter how way out someone's idea may seem, people will consider it important. It doesn't matter whether they agree with it or not." In this regard, the atmosphere in a school can be compared to the Biblical parable of the sower: "Where good ground exists, it is possible for the seeds to grow."

Intensity of Involvement

A third core quality is intensity of involvement. It doesn't really matter what the philosophy of the school is, as long as all the people in it are doing something. Where activity exists, apathy, that blight on positive effort, is not likely to be present. Creative production, whether it be poetry writing, painting, music, or whatever, comes from active involvement. On a recent teaching trip to Harvard University, I discovered a lapel button that captures this thinking in two words: DO IT.

These three qualities, then, I would rate as the necessary core for any school seeking distinctive creative output. It must be a caring place where everybody counts; it must have an atmosphere of openness about it; and it must be a doing place where people get involved.

As a complement to these three core qualities, I propose four additional elements which contribute to the atmosphere of the school:

A Framework of Discipline

Pupils must control themselves and be considerate of others. If they deviate, the class or the school is in danger of being dominated by the selfish, anti-social minority. When this occurs, the freedom of the individual is lost.

A Sense of Humour

When people enjoy what they are doing, everything seems to go better. Humour is one of the ingredients of delight, and I regard any classroom period without at least one good laugh as a failure. Young people should be encouraged to look on the light side of things, and to get as much fun as possible out of the tasks of each day. Smiles and laughter will help them to discover their best selves.

A Lively Curiosity

It is important that all of us, as we grow up, try to retain our sense of wonder, the wide eyes and amazement of our childhood. We can help to accomplish this by encouraging the inquisitive side of our nature; by asking questions as kids do and by keeping our eyes and ears open to the many miracles around us. We should fight to avoid losing what Robert Druce has aptly called "the eye of innocence."

A Knowledge of Techniques

Writing is a craft and as such, demands skills that can best be learned through instruction and practice. When pupils have been well taught, they have developed some of the tools of the writer's trade and hence are more capable of making words work for them. Yet how difficult a task this remains always, even for the most seasoned writers. Remember the answer Ernest Hemingway gave when asked by a cub reporter why he had rewritten the last paragraph of *For Whom The Bell Tolls* 39 times over. "What was your problem?" asked the naïve reporter. "My problem," replied Hemingway, with an assurance gained from years of hard-earned experience at his desk, "was getting the words right."

Any Philosophy Can Work

Obviously many other factors could be added to this list. It matters little what the philosophy of the school is, whether it be a tough Outward Bound type of place or far more relaxed. As long as the head, his staff, and pupils agree on what they are trying to achieve, and there is little ambiguity about standards, then the school with the core qualities and additional characteristics outlined above is likely to work as a creative place.

Evidently there is no one right answer as to how a creative school should be run. In fact, different countries and cultures have shown that there is a diversity of right answers as long as the basic core is sound.

The Schools

I am frequently asked to name distinguished, creative schools from all those I have visited. As a tribute to the outstanding people in these places, I shall single out 19 schools that excel in terms of the criteria I have established. I can assure you that drawing up this list was the most difficult task of all!

ASIA
Raffles Institution, Singapore

AUSTRALIA
Downlands College, Toowoomba, Queensland
Friends School, Hobart, Tasmania
The King's School, Parramatta, New South Wales
Sydney Grammar School, Sydney, New South Wales

CANADA
Dunton High School, Montreal, Quebec
Hull Elementary School, Hull, Quebec
St. John's School, Selkirk, Manitoba

EAST AFRICA
Jamhuri High School, Nairobi, Kenya

ENGLAND
Crown Woods Comprehensive School, London
The Dragon School, Oxford
Repton School, Repton, Derbyshire

FRANCE
Ecole Primaire de Val d'Isère, Savoie

SOUTH AMERICA
The Grange School, Santiago di Chile

UNITED STATES of AMERICA
Iolani School, Honolulu, Hawaii
Otter Valley High School, Brandon, Vermont
Phillips Exeter Academy, Exeter, New Hampshire
Punahou School, Honolulu, Hawaii
Putney School, Putney, Vermont

Appendix 1
More Poems

This short section contains an additional selection of poems written by pupils from many countries. I am introducing these new poems under headings corresponding to the sections in the book. You can use them for discussion purposes or simply for your and your class' enjoyment. In any case they stand as a tribute to the imaginative powers of the young.

Something to Eat

Wrinkly like a piece of well-worn leather;
Sweet with juice;
Brown with darker shades;
A tender, jammy smell
PRUNE.

(T.B., Riverdale High School, Montreal, Canada)

They're cooked in grease,
And smell like wood:
Long and narrow:
They bend your fork to smithereens
And break your teeth in two.
GREASY JOE'S FRENCH FRIES.

(K.V., Westmount High School,
Montreal, Canada)

Small pieces of meat with lots of bones;
Surrounded by a pool of sauce;
Sticky and sweet smelling;
They taste spicy, juicy, and syrupy:
CHINESE SPARE RIBS.

(T.W., Marymount High School,
Montreal, Canada)

A clumsy nervous rectangle,
Any colour at all:
Sinks when you touch it,
But always comes back in the same shape;
In your mouth,
It seems to want to run away.
JELLO.
(Alfonso Paoletti, Piux X High School,
Montreal, Canada)

Black, smoky, clouds of grey:
Hot as cloth on fire;
Grating, crumbling, awful taste
BURNT TOAST
(C.C., North Ryde High School,
North Ryde, Australia)

Distillation

Autumn

We walked through the forest
All through the day,
Gathering leaves of many colours:
On our way home,
We realized that
We had autumn in our pockets.
(D.M., Verdun High School,
Montreal, Canada)

Fear

In the doorway
A shadow—
Fear

(M.M., Cardinal Newman High School,
Montreal, Canada)

Butterfly

*How beautiful it looks;
At each stroke of its wings.
It throws a flash of golden flame.*

(Anil Posooa, St. Andrews College,
Curepipe, Mauritius)

Broken Window

*The ground has diamonds;
The mansion has none.*

(John Brett, Selwyn House School,
Montreal, Canada)

Solve a Poem

Dancing,
Fiery,
With a shiny, glistening gleam.

(Ian Watts, Blackwood High School,
Adelaide, Australia)

Answer: Opal

Invisible, strong and harmful,
Fast, swirling energy,
Sucking up the sky,
A cloud's motor.

(M. Morgan, St. Ignatius College,
Sydney, Australia)

Answer: Wind

Red, green, and sometimes gold,
Fickle;
Power in its speech.

(Linda Gibb, Dunton High School,
Montreal, Canada)

Answer: Traffic Light

Cuts like a razor,
Clear as mountain water,
Always look twice to make sure it's there.

(Maureen Gorman, Marymount High School,
Montreal, Canada)

Answer: Glass

Brightening to the eye,
Suddenly flashing
It can change your dull world,
And make it smashing.
(Debbie Cass, John Grant High School,
Montreal, Canada)

Answer: A Smile

They attract our sight,
And make even the unfortunate,
The best of poets.
(J. Belath, Royal College,
Port Louis, Mauritius)

Answer: Girls

Open Your Eyes

Fire Hydrant

You're a dog's friend,
And there's no end.
To the number of tickets
You give to cars.

(Ian Mallory,
Westmount High School,
Montreal, Canada)

Bulldozer

Your only greasy iron hands
Lock together;
Muscles of steel
Tendons of iron
Roaring.

(Steven Whalen,
Elizabeth Ballantyne School,
Montreal, Canada)

*Spider Web**

You're stuck, tangled,
Sticky, unbearable, uncomfortable,
You weave in and out;
Your heart thumps hard.

(Danny Scholtz,
Elizabeth Ballantyne School,
Montreal, Canada)

*It is interesting to note that the writer of this very sensory poem is deaf.

Pine Tree

Pine tree,
Dark sentry of the woods;
Your green boughs
Fine-laced and strong,
Stand stark against the sky—
Reach high.

(B.P., Morin Heights
Intermediate School,
Morin Heights, Canada)

Barnyard

A gathering place—
The relics
Of a forgotten past
Brought to life
For those who can see.

(K.S., St. Johnsbury Academy,
St. Johnsbury, U.S.A.)

Baffin Island

Treeless land:
Rocky flat land;
White, cold land;
Tracks of animals;
Black place.

(Sarah Levie,
Gordon Robertson Education Center,
Frobisher Bay, Canada)

Sound Variations

I Like Sounds

Truck sounds,
Train sounds,
People-talking sounds,
Men-firing-car sounds,
Building-a-building sounds;
I like sounds.

(F.P., Royal Arthur School,
Montreal, Canada)

Sportscar

As he turns on the key and lets it roar,
I wish I could drive it;
As he lets out the clutch, and begins to move,
I wish I could drive it;
As he pours on the gas, and really peals out,
I wish I could drive it.

(Rodney Guy, St. Johnsbury Academy,
St. Johnsbury, U.S.A.)

Sounds in the Morning

In the morning the alarm clock screams
Bedsprings clang;
The shower pours;
I hear bacon sizzling;
And the car engine roar,
The morning is filled with sounds.

(Luci Mathews, Coogee South Elementary School,
Sydney, Australia)

175

Portrait From the Animal World

Pick-Peter Bird

This creature always flies backwards:
Because it's been where it's going,
It doesn't care where it's going,
If it gets to where it went.

(L. Higgs, Harbour Island Public School, Bahamas)

Seagull

Immaculately white,
Travelling so high,
In the blue,
Effortlessly reaching the horizon.

(L.G., Punahou School, Honolulu, Hawaii)

Swan

Graceful, flowing, magnificent,
Is the black swan;
Its wings rustle with fast movement;
Its feathers black as the blackest night;
Such graceful motions has the swan.

(Vanessa Matson, Kapinara School, Perth, Australia)

The Magpie

The magpie's call in the morning
Like a trumpet heralds the day;
Then a streak of black and white—
And the magpie is away.

(Patrick Stephens, Downlands College,
Toowoomba, Australia)

The Leopard

Walking stealthily through the trees,
Claws curved inwards,
Eyes blazing red hot,
Tail wiping the bushes—
The leopard.

(Isaac Z., Jamhuri High School, Nairobi, Kenya)

Salmon

A jump,
A quick look around,
A flick of the tail—
Back to the depths.

(Cam McKay, St. George's School,
Vancouver, Canada)

Jersey Cow

Standing in stupid silence
A silhouette of life against the sky
Mouth moving, nose drooling
Food taste, and food waste
Without the need of latrine or hanky.

**(Denise Ryan, Downlands College,
Toowoomba, Australia)**

Portrait of Yourself

Myself

I am like a zoo of animals—
The laughter of the hyena;
The mischievousness of the monkey;
The wide-eyed wonder of the owl;
The playfulness of the cub;
The clumsiness of the bear;
The pride of the swan;
I am often caged in—
I am like a zoo of animals.

*(S.T., Macdonald High School,
Montreal, Canada)*

Myself

**I am a balloon
Blowing in the wind
Or carried by whoever
wants to bother with me;
Sometimes up,
Sometimes down,
But always full up to my ears
With whatever's floating around.**

**(R.T., Phillips Exeter Academy,
Exeter, U.S.A.)**

Contrasts

Sun/Moon

Blaring rays upon white sand;
One white flower out of a field of black.
(Sallie Collett, Putney School, Putney, U.S.A.)

Hot/Cold

Hot cocoa chasing the chill out of cold bones;
A bracing dip to wash away the sweat.
(Perry Lloyd, Putney School, Putney, U.S.A.)

Sweet/Sour

Harsh, and sending prickly chills up the cheeks;
Smooth, and putting smiles on lips.
(Kevin Calkins, Lyndon Institute, Lyndonville, U.S.A.)

Concrete/Abstract

Staring right under your nose;
Remote, seen only in dreams.
(Michael Whitehead, Selwyn House School,
Montreal, Canada)

What Interests You Most

Girlfriend

Glory be
It's she:
Oh how pretty—
Just for me.

(Stephan Stangret,
Norwood High School,
Adelaide, Australia)

Snowblower

Snow gushing outward,
Clearing and making snow fly,
Booming with pleasure.

(Peter Knight, Metis Beach School,
Metis Beach, Canada)

Paper Glider

Once just a plain sheet of paper;
White and lined like all the rest;
Now folded, moulded and unique
It glides—
Up

Up.

(J.G., Otter Valley High School,
Brandon, U.S.A.)

Adventure

Manhood Ceremony

Be strong, and bear your pain;
Thump, thump, on your back and legs:
Bear not a tear,
For that is not manly;
Heed me, little sons,
Obey your elders;
For the ceremonial to manhood is hard;
Be strong and tough through the hardship
That the elders give to be a man.
(P.S., Garoka High School,
Garoka, Papua New Guinea)

Why Quit?

Why stop now?
Why quit?
You have everything to gain—
Nothing to lose;
Keep going;
Keep being;
Keep learning;
Why stop now?
(J.B., St. George's School,
Montreal, Canada)

Bull-riding

Up, down,
Flat on my butt;
On again,
Off again,
Do it some more.
(T.M., Hawaii Preparatory Academy,
Kamuela, Hawaii)

Wargaming*

Miniatures in millions,
Across the table they swarm,
Marching to their foe
Like ants heading for a jam jar.
(Jeremy Shrimpton, Canford School,
Dorset, England)

*Wargaming is an intricate and demanding pastime popular wlth English
schoolboys at the moment.

The Greatest Word in the World

Love

Love is not an engagement
ring from Angus and Coote;
Or eating something special
with another being;
Love is sharing one's innermost feelings,
With one who understands.

(A.T., The King's School, Parramatta, Australia)

Celebration

Chanukah*

Chanukah, Chanukah,
Festival of lights,
Spin the little dreidel,
And get a menorah to light;
Eat a lot of latkes,
Give a lot of gifts,
Sing a lot of songs,
And you'll make happiness:
Have a family gathering,
Say a lot of blessings,
Think a lot about Jerusalem,
And the Miracle that happened.

(David Levy, Lower Canada College,
Montreal, Canada)

*Chanukah is the Jewish celebration of the festival of lights.

Appendix 2
Participating Schools

Australian Schools

NEW SOUTH WALES
Coogee South Elementary School, Coogee South
Cranbrook School, Bellevue Hill
The King's School, Parramatta
Marist Brothers College, Dundas
North Ryde High School, North Ryde
Pittwater House Grammar School, Collaroy
St. Ignatius College, Riverview
Santa Sabena Convent, Strathfield
Scots College, Bellevue Hill
Sydney Grammar School

QUEENSLAND
Brisbane Grammar School, Brisbane
Christian Brothers College, Warwick
Downlands College, Toowoomba
Warwick High School, Warwick

SOUTH AUSTRALIA
Blackwood High School, Adelaide
Girton Girls School, Adelaide
Norwood High School, Adelaide
Scotch College, Adelaide

TASMANIA
Friends School, Hobart
Rosetta High School, Hobart

VICTORIA
Marcellin College, Bulleen
Peninsula School, Mt. Eliza

WESTERN AUSTRALIA
Kapinara School, Perth
Marist College, Churchlands, Perth
Marist School, Bunbury

Canada

Montreal Schools

Cardinal Newman High School
Dorval High School, Dorval
Dunton High School
Elizabeth Ballantyne School
John Grant High School
Lachine High School, Lachine
Lower Canada College
Macdonald High School, Ste. Anne de Bellevue
Macdonald College of Education
Marymount High School
Monklands High School
Monseigneur Doran High School
Montreal West High School
Mount Royal High School
Outremont High School
Pius X High School, Montreal North
Riverdale High School, Pierrefonds
Royal Arthur School
St. George's School
Selwyn House School
Sir Winston Churchill High School
Thomas d'Arcy McGee Annex
Verdun High School
Wagar High School
West Hill High School
Westmount High School

Other Canadian Schools

BRITISH COLUMBIA
Caribou Hill Secondary School, Burnaby
St. George's School, Vancouver
York House School, Vancouver

MANITOBA
Brandon Collegiate Institute, Brandon
Elton Collegiate Institute, Forest
Neelin High School, Brandon
Park School, Brandon
St. John's School, Selkirk

NORTHWEST TERRITORIES
Gordon Robertson Educational Center, Frobisher Bay

ONTARIO
University of Toronto School, Toronto

QUEBEC
Bishop's College School, Lennoxville
Gatineau Elementary School, Gatineau
Hull Elementary School, Hull
Metis Beach School, Metis Beach
Morin Heights Intermediate School, Morin Heights
Philaemon Wright High School, Hull, Quebec

SASKATCHEWAN
Central High School, Moose Jaw
Central High School, Regina
Mount Royal High School, Saskatoon
St. Michael's School, Moose Jaw

English Schools

Ashfield School, Nottingham
Bilton Grange School, Dunchurch
Bryanston School, Dorset
Canford School, Dorset
Casterton School, Kirkby Lonsdale, Cumbria
Crown Woods Comprehensive School, London
The Dragon School, Oxford
Foremark School, Repton, Derbyshire
Illminster Grammar School, Somerset
King's School, Ely, Cambridgeshire
Repton School, Derbyshire
Sandroyd School, Tollard Royal, Wiltshire
Sherbourne School, Somerset
Winchester College, Hampshire

Schools in Other Countries

BAHAMAS
Harbour Island Public School, Harbour Island
St. Benedict's School, Harbour Island

CHILE
The Grange School, Santiago

FRANCE
Ecole Primaire de Val d'Isère, Savoie

KENYA
Jamhuri High School, Nairobi

MAURITIUS
Loretto Convent, Quatre Bornes
Loretto Convent, St. Pierre
Royal College, Curepipe
Royal College, Port Louis
St. Andrew's College, Curepipe

NEPAL
St. Paul's School, Darjeeling

PAPUA NEW GUINEA
Garoka Teacher's College, Garoka

SINGAPORE
Raffles Institution

U.S.S.R.
School 52, Moscow

United States Schools

CALIFORNIA
Carmel High School, Carmel

HAWAII
Hawaii Preparatory Academy, Kamuela
Iolani School, Honolulu
Kahehameha School, Honolulu
Punahou School, Honolulu

MASSACHUSETTS
Belmont Hill School, Boston
Harvard School of Education, Cambridge
Newton High School, Boston

NEW HAMPSHIRE
Phillips Exeter Academy, Exeter

NEW YORK
Horace Mann School, Yonkers

VERMONT
Forest Dale School, Forest Dale
Lyndon Institute, Lyndonville
Otter Valley High School, Brandon
Putney School, Putney
St. Johnsbury Academy, St. Johnsbury

Index